KIDS EXPLORE

FLORIDA

Includes:
Walt Disney World
Busch Gardens
Universal Studios
Spaceport USA
and much more

Susan D. Moffat

Bob Adams, Inc.
Holbrook, Massachusetts

Published by Bob Adams, Inc.
260 Center Street, Holbrook, MA 02343

ISBN: 1-55850-439-7

Printed in Korea

J   I   H   G   F   E   D   C   B   A

Library of Congress Cataloging-in-Publication Data
Moffat, Susan D.
    Kids explore Florida : includes Disney World, Busch Gardens, Universal
Studios, Spaceport USA, and much more / Susan D. Moffat.
        p.   cm.
    Includes index.
    ISBN 1-55850-427-3
    1. Florida—Guidebooks. 2. Children—Travel—Florida—Guidebooks. 3.
Family recreation—Florida—Guidebooks. I. Title
    F309.3.M64   1994
    917.5904'63—dc20   94-33645
                                                                      CIP

This publication is designed to provide accurate and authoritative information with regard to
the subject matter covered. It is sold with the understanding that the publisher is not engaged
in rendering legal, accounting, or other professional advice. If legal advice or other expert
assistance is required, the services of a competent professional person should be sought.
  — From a *Declaration of Principles* jointly adopted by a Committee of the American Bar
                              Association and a Committee of Publishers and Associations

Cover design: Peter Gouck
Front cover and interior photos: Susan D. Moffat (except where noted)
Rear cover photo: Laf Reid

*This book is available at quantity discounts for bulk purchases.
For information, call 1-800-872-5627.*

In Memory of My Mother and Father

ACKNOWLEDGMENTS

My thanks go out to the many people who helped me along the way and made this book possible—the public relations departments and directors of the many sites; Rick Dey, for his patience and editing expertise; Peter Gouck for putting it all together; Nancy Malone, the C.H. Moffats, and Laf Reid for their kind hospitality and escape from the alligators and shuttle launches; Tami Monahan for being a computer aficionado; Denny Williams for keeping Akihiro; Sara Jacobson and Bob Lacey. Each provided support in many ways—from providing me with a bed to feeding my dog while I was away.

TABLE OF CONTENTS

4

INTRODUCTION

I wrote and photographed *Kids Explore Florida* to reveal the best places for you and your kids to experience in Florida, and to provide comprehensive, accurate information to make your explorations in the "Sunshine State" smoother and more pleasurable.

From coast to coast, Florida is vast and variable. It's a state loaded with history, simulation, and a mix of cultures. Where else can you find Barbie going on a safari in exotic lands, Jaws consuming tour boats in a single gulp, real satellites taking off for outer space, and manatees chomping on lettuce heads as they play in the water?

While practically everyone on this planet has heard of Walt Disney World, and for good reason, there *is* more to Florida. There are wonderful science, art, and history museums which encourage learning through hands-on, interactive activities and exhibits. There are also a number of zoos, aquaria, and parks. And there is an expansive coastline with sandy beaches galore.

It's a state loaded with theme parks and recreational activities of every kind for people of all ages–not just kids. In my mind, if a family has the means to take a trip to Florida during the kids' growing-up years, they should.

You may feel the need to "jam it all into one visit" in order to achieve maximum satisfaction. Don't! Instead, I would suggest looking over the free brochures available at most of the major sites and selecting exhibits or displays that most interest you. *Kids Explore Florida* will give you ideas of what to expect.

The best, and really only, way of getting around Florida is by car, which partially explains why Orlando has the largest rental car market in the USA. Some of the bigger hotels in Orlando do provide transportation to Walt Disney World, Universal Studios, and Sea World. You should plan to purchase maps. One I found particularly useful, and free, can be obtained from Florida's Division of Tourism (126 Van Buren Street, Tallahassee, Florida 32399. Telephone: 904/487-1462).

Safety is always an issue, of course. Contrary to what the media might lead you to believe, the infamous "drive-by shootings" and "car-jackings" of tourists are rare. However, there are some precautions which you might take while using a rental or out-of-state car. Consider, for example, disguising your vehicle. The car will blend in more easily if you tone it down by using bumper stickers, or hanging some fuzzy dice or rosary beads from the rear-view mirror.

A word of warning: Although I was careful to be very accurate about admission prices and hours, they do tend to change. You might want to call to confirm them.

Putting this book together has been a true adventure. I hope you and your kids enjoy exploring Florida as much as I did. Happy exploration!

Susan D. Moffat

FUN SCALE

These balloon ratings are the result of a number of factors, including: How long will the attraction hold your child's attention? Does it have educational value? Will it make the children smile or laugh? Is it interactive and hands-on? Is the price of admission fair? Are the facilities safe? Are they well maintained and appropriately supervised? Is it a site where both parents and children can find interest and have fun? Only those which score highest in these areas of consideration are five-ballooners!

 One Balloon–Not worth any extra energy to get there; but, if you do happen to be in the neighborhood, you might take a gander.

 Two Balloons–Not the most fun place on the planet for kids, but it has some redeeming qualities.

 Three Balloons–A middle-of-the-road site on the fun scale, but worth a visit.

 **Four Balloons**–Great place, and well worth a visit.

 **Five Balloons**–Holy cow! The ultimate in fun and definitely not to be missed.

ICON EXPLANATION

Wheelchair Accessible

Restaurant

Picnicking

Rest Rooms

Gift Shop

"BEST OF" RATINGS

Very few of the sites are limited to one specific age range. With a few exceptions, most of the "five ballooners" cover a variety of activities which span the age range. The exceptions are listed in parenthesis next to the sites below.

Aerial Adventures of Orlando (8 and up)
American Police Hall of Fame (8 and up)
Brevard Zoo (10 and younger)
Busch Gardens
EPCOT Center (8 and up)
Great Explorations
Lion Country Safari
Lowry Park Zoo
Magic Kingdom
MGM Studios Theme Park
Museum of Science and Discovery
Orlando Science Center (4 and up)
Sea World
St. Augustine's Alligator Farm
Universal Studios
Venetian Pool

WALT DISNEY WORLD
Guest Information
P.O. Box 10040
Lake Buena Vista, FL 32830
(407) 824-4321

From Mickey to Barbie, from Daffy to Ninja Turtles, from a pastry in France to "Illuminations" exploding in the sky, Disney World, as a whole, can be mind-bogglingly humongous. Even broken down by theme park, it's somewhat overwhelming. So, it's important to familiarize yourself with what's out there before venturing into the world of Disney. Scan through the Disney World section and see what most interests you. Because each of the parks is so large, I've highlighted only what I consider the "best of" in each one. Maps, which are provided free at each park, will help. Take your time, and don't forget–have fun!

ADMISSIONS

	Age 10+	Ages 3-9 (under 3 free)
One-day, one-park ticket (to Magic Kingdom OR EPCOT OR MGM Studios)	$35.00	$28.00
* Four-Day Value Pass	125.00	98.00
** Five-Day Around the World Pass	170.00	135.00
*** Theme Park Annual Pass	199.00	174.00
River Country 1-Day	14.00	11.00
River Country Annual	52.50	52.50
Discovery Island	9.50	5.25
River Country/Discovery Isl. Combo.	16.75	12.25
Typhoon Lagoon 1-Day	20.50	16.50
Typhoon Lagoon Annual	78.75	78.75

* Provides one day at Magic Kingdom, one day at EPCOT, one day at MGM Studios, and one day at guest's choice of one park; good any four days following purchase.
** Provides one day at Magic Kingdom, one day at EPCOT, one day at MGM, two days of guest's choice of one park each day; also includes admission to Typhoon Lagoon, River Country, Discovery Island, and Pleasure Island for a period of seven days beginning with the first date stamped (first use).
*** Provides unlimited admission to MGM Studios, EPCOT and Magic Kingdom for one year from date of voucher redemption.
Strollers are available for rent.

MAGIC KINGDOM
Walt Disney World
(407) 824-4321

FUN SCALE

Magic Kingdom is what most people think of when they think of Disney World, and it's home to such Disney greats as Mickey Mouse, Donald Duck, the Country Bear Jamboree, and the notorious Space Mountain ride.

Begin in the **Town Square** and pick up an information booklet and map in the **City Hall**. Sit down, spread the map out, and plan your day. You might need to sit on the kids because, if they're like most, they'll be off and running at full-tilt toward **Space Mountain** as soon as the gates open. Look up at **Cinderella's Castle**; it's a good landmark. The Magic Kingdom is divided into different subkingdoms all radiating from the Castle–Fantasyland, Mickey's Starland, Tomorrowland, Adventureland, Frontierland, and Liberty Square.

Experience the magic of **Fantasyland**. Submerge, via submarine at *20,000 Leagues Under the Sea*, and travel past underwater

volcanoes, seahorses, and even mermaids. (Fun for anyone not likely to feel claustrophobic.) Engage in a *Mad Tea Party* while you sit in giant pink teacups on giant pink saucers tilting and whirling frantically around. Board the boat and sing to the beat of "It's a Small World" as you travel around the globe experiencing cute Disneyish cultures. (Sweet at any age.) Don't miss *Magic Journey*, the fifteen-minute long, 3-D film that follows the imagination of five children. You're taken over mountaintops, confronted by a kite that's heading straight for you, and have dandelion spores blown in your face–all through 3-D glasses. (Inspirational at any age.)

Mickey's Starland is a must for young Mickey Mouse fans. Step into Mickey's dressing room and have your photo taken with the mouse himself. Say "cheese!" The main attraction is *Mickey's Starland Show*. Groove to the tunes with characters including Chip 'n' Dale Rescue Rangers, Baloo, and Goofy and his son. It's a cute, sing-along, musical comedy that young kids go wild over. (Wonderful for ages seven and under.)

The most popular section (hands down) of **Tomorrowland** is *Space Mountain*. This is made obvious when the gates of Disney World open and a vacuum-effect is left after the kids rush toward the 180-foot-high futuristic structure serving to house the cosmic roller coaster. Board the rocket and blast–rising, crashing, and zipping along at startlingly-fast speeds in the dark–through space and past galaxies. The ride lasts for only two and one-half minutes, but the memory lasts much longer. A word to the wise–don't eat right beforehand. (Children under eight might find the ride too scary. I did!)

Pirate fans head straight for **Adventureland**, and search for *Pirates of the Caribbean*. Ahoy mates! This is a favorite among young buccaneers and one not to miss. The boat ride takes you leisurely through dark spaces, in which you are surrounded by life-like figures of pirates in brothels and jails, and by loads of hidden bounty. (It might be a little scary for ages four and under.) Another nautically-themed favorite is the *Jungle Cruise*. Board the open-air boat and take a trip through four distant lands, ranging from an Asian jungle to

11

an Amazon rain forest. You'll see hippos, lions, giraffes, and even headhunters with spears. And it's all narrated by a captain with a lot of corny but nevertheless funny jokes. (A great family ride, though possibly not much fun for teens.)

The atmosphere in **Frontierland** is one of hee-haw, frontier-style fun. Log cabins, cowboy clothing, and a scrubby western landscape set the stage for activities such as a good ol' *Country Bear Jamboree*. Get down with the slap-happy, ukulele strummin', footstompin' bears. Sit down and let the toothless musicians serenade you with heart-warming tunes–a nice break from the moving rides. (Perfect for all ages.) For something more action-oriented, a ride down *Splash Mountain* might be just the solution. Start off slowly, passing figures of cute rabbits, birds, and frogs, all to the tune of goofy songs like "Skip to My Lou My Darling." Floating unsuspectingly along, you're thrown, plummeting fifty-two feet over a vertical drop, into a watery briar patch. Kids love to throw their arms overhead and scream all the way down. (It's short but sweet, and sure to appeal to thrill seekers, but may be too much for kids under seven. Heed the physical limitation warnings and get set to get wet, especially if you're sitting in the front.) *Big Thunder Mountain Railroad* offers another frontier-themed, roller-coasterish ride–minus the water. Board the runaway mine train and travel through the convincing scenery of a derelict old mining town, complete with possums, donkeys, chickens, and even a grizzly old miner caught soaking in the tub. (Much tamer than Splash Mountain and okay for any age, but you should still heed the physical limitations warnings.)

Enter **Liberty Square** and experience eighteenth-century, colonial America. It's a small transitional area between Fantasyland and Frontierland, consisting of stately architecture and neatly manicured lawns. The *Hall of Presidents* provides a thirty-minute, multimedia experience, along with a view of the Audio-Animatronics robotic figures of all of the presidents, from George

Washington to Bill Clinton. Who will be the next addition? (Any age will benefit by the educational experience.) The favorite in Liberty Square is the eight-minute *Haunted Mansion* adventure. Special effects make it a chilling ride as you slide past tombstones, forever-appearing ravens, and awesome ghosts. (Because there are a few periods of total darkness, it might be too scary for children under eight.)

Whatever you do, don't miss the **3:00 P.M. Parade**. It's thirty minutes long and characters like Mickey Mouse, Donald Duck, and Snow White are sure to delight as they begin parading on Main Street and continue through Frontierland and Liberty Square. The music is lively, people are dancing, and everyone's having a wonderful time. Make sure to stake out a good viewing spot about a half-an-hour beforehand. It's worth the wait.

Age Range: Most ages will find pleasure. See comments above.
Hours: Sunday through Thursday from 8:00 A.M. to 12:00 midnight, Friday and Saturday from 8:00 A.M. to 11:00 P.M.
Admission: See chart on page 9 under Walt Disney World.
Time Allowance: Full day.
Directions: From I-4 take Exit 25 and follow the signs.
Parking: $5.00 per day.
Wheelchair Accessible: Yes.
Restaurant: Yes, many.
Picnicking: No.
Rest Rooms: Yes, with changing tables.
Gift Shop: Yes, many, with all kinds of Disney memorabilia.
Cool Tip: Animal boarding facilities available for a fee.

EPCOT CENTER
Walt Disney World
(407) 824-4321

FUN SCALE

Walt Disney hungered for a model world where nations live at peace. He chose Orlando as the site and built EPCOT Center (Experimental Prototype City of Tomorrow) to make his dream come true. It is made up of two parts, Future World and World Showcase. EPCOT as a whole is huge (30,000 acres–twice the size of Manhattan), and the need to give some forethought to your itinerary is important. You may even plan to spend two days taking EPCOT in at a slower pace.

FUTURE WORLD puts Disney's vision to work with innovative exhibits and rides focusing on yesterday, today, and tomorrow through ten theme pavilions.

As you enter EPCOT you'll see, rising seventeen stories high and centered inside the identifiable giant silver ball, **Spaceship Earth**. Learn about the history of communications as you're taken on a fifteen-minute journey, via "time machine," from Cro-Magnon man to the present. Travel slowly past stars and planets, dinosaurs, cave men and cave paintings, hieroglyphics, a Greek theater, the first printing press of the Renaissance days, and the Sistine Chapel ceiling, all the way up to the electronic communications of TV, videos, and computers. (It's fun for age eight and up.)

Journey into Imagination is divided into two floors of excitement. Downstairs includes *Captain EOM*, a seventeen-minute film starring Michael Jackson and Angelica Houston; and the "Journey into Imagination Ride," a fourteen-minute adventure into the exploration of the dreams of Figment, a baby dragon. Climb upstairs and check out *Image Works.* (I guarantee you won't be sorry.) It's an interactive playspace full of hands-on electronic gismos to tap into that creative side of all of us. (Great for any age.)

Explore the deep of **The Living Seas** and see the world's "sixth ocean," the largest aquarium in existence. Living in it are over five thousand sea creatures–barracuda, sharks, sea lions, rays, and dolphins. Take the three-minute *Coral Reef Ride* and circumnavigate the giant tank. The ride ends at *Seabase Alpha*, where you'll see a model of an ocean-research facility of the future. Now's your chance to look closely at the sea creatures and try out some of the hands-on exhibits. Put on a diving suit and pretend you're in the ocean. (Fun for any age.)

The Wonders of Life takes a light and educationally healthy look at fitness, health, and the human body, and is another "don't miss." *The Making of Me* is a wonderful fifteen-minute film narrated by Martin Short. It's a humorous but sensitive skit touching on those age-old questions concerning where babies come from. (Five and up will benefit from and be entertained by the film.) In *Cranium Command* you're placed inside the brain of Buzzy, an Audio Animatronic, in a multimedia presentation. Learn about what goes on in the mind of a twelve year old during the normal course of the day. (Yikes! This is good for age eight and up.) *Body Wars* is another favorite among kids. It's a five minute simulated rough and bumpy ride through the human body. (This may be too much jerking for young children–it was for me!) For some hands-on activity, step out into the interactive *Fitness Pavilion*. There are tons of hands-on activities that challenge and educate people of all ages about the wonders of life.

The Universe of Energy, although it has some amazing special effects, seems too drawn out. However, the giant Audio Animatronic dinosaurs

surrounded by Mesozoic Era steam and fog, lightening, and dinosaurs screaming, are entertaining. (Children of any age, especially eight and under, will find this too long.)

The Land pavilion deals with everyone's favorite topic of conversation–food. Six acres are dedicated to this cherished subject, and you can easily spend a couple of hours here. *Listen to the Land* takes you on a thirteen-minute boatride through a rain forest, a prairie, and a desert. See how plants grow in such extreme environments. *Symbiosis* is a twenty-minute National Geographic film that touches on the necessary balance between modern technology and the fragile environment. Brilliant camera work covers scenes from the Hoover Dam to the pastoral farmland of the midwest. The message is clear–there is a need for a balance–and the film ends on a positive note. On a the lighter side, you might want to step into the *Kitchen Kabaret*. Bonnie Appetite takes you through twelve minutes of Audio Animatronics with dancing fruits and vegetables–Mexican mariachi style! (Any age will enjoy the boatride in *Listen to the Land* and the light atmosphere of *Kitchen Kabaret*. Save *Symbiosis* for kids ten years and older.)

Just beyond Future World lies the **WORLD SHOWCASE**–Disney's dream come true, bringing people together from different nations of the planet to share their cultures. Enter and experience a trip around the globe. Taste the foods, talk to the people, and take in the demonstrations, films and exhibits of eleven miniaturized nations: Canada, the United Kingdom, France, Japan, the USA, Italy, Germany, China, Mexico, Morocco, and Norway. Don't forget to buy a **passport** at any World Showcase Shop. Get it stamped in each country you visit. It's a great souvenir.

Beginning with something close to home, **American Adventure** takes you on a thirty-minute tour via Ben Franklin and Mark Twain Audio-Animatronic figures. From the Pilgrims landing at Plymouth Rock to present day events, you're taken through history. Outside, make sure you catch a Barbie Show. *The Magical World of Barbie* is scheduled throughout the day and a "must" for Barbie fans. It's live (with *real* people), and Barbie is hip, cool, and *so* fashionable. She and her friends surf, dance, and safari through a foreign country–right before your eyes! (Eight and up will enjoy the American Adventure. Ten and under will go nuts over Barbie.)

A favorite of the kids' is **Norway's Adventure of the Sea**, the five-minute Maelstrom ride through Norwegian history. Dragon-headed Viking boats take you through shipyards and forests with three-headed trolls, and then they head straight for a dangerous waterfall. (Might be too scary for young children.)

Warning: Canada offers such a wonderful eighteen-minute film called **O Canada!** that you may just decide to pack up and move to Canada. Completely surround yourself with the 360-degree CircleVision screen, and take in views from the pristine and colorful city of Montreal to a dog sled being led through the snowy countryside. It's a patriotic panorama that leaves you breathless. There are no seats in the theater–you stand throughout. (Ten and

16

up will appreciate the patriotism.)

If you're hungry, head for the Eiffel Tower landmark and visit France. Grab a pastry and step into **Impression de France**, the eighteen-minute movie shown on a 200-degree screen. Sit back and take a tour through the French Alps, Parisian palaces, and country vineyards at harvest time. (Ten and up will appreciate the movie. Any age will appreciate the food.)

Don't miss the spectacular **IlluminNations** high-tech light show. It's fifteen-minutes of fireworks, darting laser beams, and strobe lights dancing before your eyes. The marvelous show takes place over the central lagoon and happens nightly, one-half hour before closing time. (Great for any age.)

Age Range: Most ages will find pleasure. See comments above.
Hours: Sunday through Thursday from 9:00 A.M. to 10:00 P.M., Friday and Saturday from 9:00 A.M. to 9:00 P.M.
Admission: See chart on page 9 under Walt Disney World.
Time Allowance: Full day.
Directions: From I-4 take Exit 26B and follow the signs.
Parking: $5.00 per day.
Wheelchair Accessible: Yes.
Restaurant: Yes, many.
Picnicking: No.
Rest Rooms: Yes, with changing tables.
Gift Shop: Yes, many, with all kinds of Disney memorabilia.

MGM STUDIOS THEME PARK
Walt Disney World
(407) 824-4321

FUN SCALE

Go behind the scenes for a day, see how animation and special effects are achieved, and experience movies and TV actually in production at MGM Studios. Don't forget to pick up an entertainment schedule and pre-plan your day. It's easy to get temporarily lost, so don't lose your map.

Lights, camera, action–Indiana Jones dramatically free falls into the Cairo setting and begins the **Indiana Jones Stunt Spectacular.** The thirty-minute high-action show uses stunt men and women to demonstrate falls from towers, tumbling from rooftops, and recuperating from being crushed by giant balls. Adult volunteers are chosen to participate as "extras" during the show. (Entertaining for all but five and younger.)

Is there such a thing as a real-live mermaid? Ariel, the animated female sea creature, is joined by fluorescent fish and a fantastically evil, octopus woman, and they're surrounded by steam from the sea, sprinkling rain, and stars from above in **Voyage of the Little Mermaid**. There often is a long line midday, so go in the early morning or late afternoon to avoid the wait. It's a cute fifteen-minute stage show, but are the mermaids live or simulated? (Wonderful for any age.)

Jim Henson's Muppet Vision 3-D is an action-packed thirty-minute performance which plays with visual effects. It's hard to tell which characters are real and which are on screen. All the Muppets make the scene, entertaining you with fireworks, cream pies, floating bubbles, and high winds.

Be sure to duck as Kermit comes at you on a ladder–right off the screen. (Fun for all ages, although teens might think it's too silly.)

Little kids need an energy outlet? The perfect solution is to step inside the **Honey, I Shrunk the Kids Movie Set Adventure**. It's a humongous recreation of the backyard in the movie, *Honey, I Shrunk the Kids.* Walk under the giant leaky hose–but be careful, it squirts from different spots each time. Hide behind thirty-foot blades of grass. Slide down the gigantic film reel. Climb around in the oversized spider web. (Fun for children eight and under.)

Strap yourself into your seat and engage in **Star Tours**, a seven-minute flight based on the *Star Wars* trilogy. Piloted by R2D2, you're rocketed through deep space past giant ice crystals, stars, and planets. In general, lines are long; but they are shorter in the morning and late afternoon. Go in with an empty stomach. (The simulated ride is semi-intense and possibly overwhelming for children under eight years.)

Turtle fans shouldn't miss the chance for a view of the awesome **Teenage Mutant Ninja Turtles**. See the bodacious crime fighters dance on stage, and be sure to cop a signature and photo afterward. Cowabunga, dude! (Great for any Turtle fan.)

Don't miss the **Aladdin Royal Caravan**. All of the favorite characters parade through the grounds from the Main Entrance Plaza, down Hollywood Boulevard, ending at Star Tours. It lasts for only ten minutes, making it a short but sweet affair. Check your schedule for the time. (A festive ten minutes for any age.)

Age Range: In general, MGM is more geared toward the younger children and older adults. See comments after each site.
Hours: Friday and Saturday from 9:00 A.M. to 9:00 P.M., Sunday through Thursday from 9:00 A.M. to 10:00 P.M. Hours can change. Call first.
Admission: See chart on page 9 under Walt Disney World.
Time Allowance: Full day.
Directions: From I-4 take Exit 25 and follow the signs.
Parking: $5.00 per day.
Wheelchair Accessible: Yes.
Restaurant: Yes, many.
Picnicking: No.
Rest Rooms: Yes, with changing tables.
Gift Shop: Yes, many, with all kinds of Disney memorabilia.

19

DISCOVERY ISLAND
Walt Disney World
(407) 824-3784

FUN SCALE

Often overshadowed by the theme parks, Discovery Island offers a chance to experience eleven and one-half acres with 120 species including birds, small primates, and reptiles. There's nothing simulated about Discovery Island–no thrilling rides, no sensationalism, just pure nature. Take a short boat ride from the Contemporary Resort, disembark, and you're surrounded by a zoological park featuring over 250 species of plants and animals. Walk through the lush stands of tropical foliage in the extensively netted aviary and see exotic birds flying freely. The roseate spoonbill is especially impressive with its spoon shaped beak. Speaking of beaks, check out the one on the rhinoceros hornbill. Its purpose is to help in catching fruit, insects, and small animals.

Spot the dazzling scarlet ibis and the blindingly-brilliant American flamingos. Put on your sunglasses! Check out the gigantic and slow-moving Galapagos tortoises. These giants can weigh as much as 500 pounds and live for 150 years. Holy turtles!

Don't miss the Animal Encounter Shows. **Feathered Friends** features a colorful parrot show with macaws and cockatoos. **Birds of Prey** offers an informative demonstration with exotic and native predatory birds, including a bald eagle and hairy vulture. You'll meet alligators and snakes in **Reptile Relations** through an educational and fun show.

During the summer, children between eight and fourteen years can partake in **Kidventure,** a four-hour summer ecology program where you'll journey through marshes, swamps, and exotic jungles, and come eye-to-eye with everything from toucans to turtles.

It's a learning experience. Call ahead for times and prices.

Age Range: While nothing is hands-on on the island, close-up views maintain the interest of all ages.
Hours: *Winter*–10:00 A.M. to 5:00 P.M., daily. Last launch at 3:45 P.M. *Summer*–10:00 A.M. to 6:00 P.M., daily. Last launch at 4:45 P.M.
Admission: See chart on page #9 under Walt Disney World.
Time Allowance: 2 to 3 hours.
Directions: From I-4 follow signs for the Magic Kingdom. Past the toll plaza move to the far right, follow signs for Contemporary Resort, and park in their lot. Board the boat for the island.
Parking: $5.00 per day.
Wheelchair Accessible: Yes, but bumpy in spots.
Restaurant: Yes.
Picnicking: Yes.
Rest Rooms: Yes, one with and one without changing tables.
Gift Shop: Yes; tote bags, cool T-shirts, and rubber insects.

TYPHOON LAGOON
Walt Disney World
(407) 560-4073

FUN SCALE

This ramshackle, Swiss Family Robinsonish, tin-roofed, island village landscaped with cargo, surfboards and other marine wreckage left by great storms sets the scene for Typhoon Lagoon. The fifty-six acre site includes such challenges as the world's largest manmade **watershed mountain** with eight twisting-and-turning waterslides and roaring streams. A two-and-one-half acre, wave-making **lagoon** features surf-size waves up to six-feet tall. The **saltwater pool** provides snorkelers with a chance to come face-to-face with multicolored creatures from the Caribbean. The biggest and fastest water slide is **Humunga Cowabunga** where you'll drop down the mountain and go rushing through a cave at speeds of up to twenty five miles per hour. Rafting adventures are available on **Castaway Creek**. **Ketchakiddee Creek** is the spot for young children to let loose and play in geysers, fountains, and a pint-sized, white-water, rafting adventure.

Age Range: Water lovers of all ages.
Hours: 10:00 A.M. to 5:00 P.M., daily. *Summer* (June through August)–9:00 A.M. to 8:00 P.M., daily.
Admission: See chart on page 9 under Walt Disney World.
Time Allowance: 3 hours to full day.
Directions: From I-4 take Exit 26B (Disney Village) and follow the signs.
Parking: Free.
Wheelchair Accessible: Yes, to a certain extent–there are boards leading to the rides.
Restaurant: Yes.

Picnicking: Yes, but no glass containers or alcoholic beverages.
Rest Rooms: Yes.
Gift Shop: Yes; bathing suits, towels, and T-shirts.

RIVER COUNTRY
Walt Disney World
(407) 824-2760

FUN SCALE

Less splashy than Typhoon Lagoon, River Country has a different sort of atmosphere, one right out of a Mark Twain novel. The swimming hole is similar to the ones Tom and Huck used to visit, with some added Disney touches. The **Ol' Swimmin' Hole** consists of ropes and ships' booms from which to swing and drop into the water below.

Whoop-N-Holler Hollow is the most popular attraction. It has two water slides which take the riders down long, winding chutes and end with a big splash. The **Ol' Wading Pool**, a pint-size version of the Ol' Swimmin' Hole, is designed for younger children who can play on its beach or in its calmer waters.

Age Range: Any age.
Hours: 10:00 A.M. to 5:00 P.M., daily. *Summer* 10:00 A.M. to 7:00 P.M., daily.
Admission: See chart on page 9 under Walt Disney World. Lockers and towels available for fee.
Time Allowance: 3 hours to full day.
Directions: From I-4 take Exit 26B and follow signs for River Country.
Parking: $5.00 per day.
Wheelchair Accessible: Yes, around the pools.
Restaurant: Snackbar only.
Picnicking: Yes, but no glass containers or alcoholic beverages.
Rest Rooms: Yes, with changing tables.
Gift Shop: Yes; T-shirts, towels, sunglasses.

AERIAL ADVENTURES OF ORLANDO
3529 Edgewater Drive
Orlando, FL 32804
(407) 841-8787

FUN SCALE

Copyright © Church Street Station

Make that balloon flying dream come true. See central Florida from a close-up, aerial perspective. Unlike most of the Orlando attractions, a ride in a hot air balloon involves no simulation or imitation of any kind. It's an exhilaratingly real and uplifting (literally) experience.

Your day begins with a wake up call at 4:30 A.M.–yikes! Meet the group at Church Street Station at 6:00 A.M. Drive–via the "chase car"–to the launch

site, which is determined by the weather. Check the wind conditions. Inflate the gigantic balloon. Get a brief lesson on safety and on the landing technique from the pilot. Climb aboard. And you're off!

You're floating above the Earth over luscious citrus groves, cotton fields, housing developments, lakes, and, if the wind is right, Disney World. Altitude varies, but at times you're close enough to be tempted to reach down and pick a tangerine from one of the trees. The hour-long experience is peaceful and quiet–except, of course, for the occasional blasts of hot air into the balloon; but, hey, they're

24

necessary to stay afloat!

Following the flight, you'll go back to the Church Street Station and be served a scrumptious champagne brunch of oj, coffee, champagne, eggs, bacon, home fries, fresh fruit, croissants, and a mint.

You'll leave with an uplifted and invigorated feeling–and a full stomach.

Age Range: 7 and up. A younger child, too short to see over the basket's edge, would have to be held by a parent, and this is considered unsafe. Parents of balloon riders can trail below in the "chase vehicle" and join them for breakfast afterward.
Hours: Wake-up call at 4:30 A.M. Brunch ends at about 10:00 A.M.
Admission: Adults $150.00 each, children (under 12) $75.00 each.
Time Allowance: 5 hours.
Directions: From I-4 take the Anderson Street Exit and turn left on Boone Avenue. Take another left on South Street, then turn right on Garland Avenue. Parking is on your right.
Parking: Lot at Church Street Station. Price included in fee.
Wheelchair Accessible: No.

Restaurant: Yes.
Picnicking: No.
Rest rooms: At Church Street Station only.
Gift Shop: No.
Cool Tip: Wear comfortable clothes and expect it to be a little cooler up above than below.

25

GATORLAND
14501 South Orange Blossom Trail
(U.S. 441)
Orlando, FL 32837
(407) 855-5496

FUN SCALE

If you're curious about alligators, Florida is the place for you. There are gator farms throughout the state, but the one to visit in the Orlando area is Gatorland. You can't miss the giant gator jaws as you travel down Route 441. Walk through the jaws entryway, and through the gift shop (of course), and you're surrounded by members of the Crocodilian order. Gatorland features five thousand alligators and crocodiles throughout the fifty-acre park.

Three shows run regularly through the day. The **Gator Jumparoo Show** is a favorite and shouldn't be missed. See alligators jump up and out of the

water to retrieve raw chicken or other delicacies right from the trainer's hand. The **Snakes of Florida Show** in the Snake Pit offers information about the poisonous and non-poisonous snakes of the Sunshine State. Watch the brave trainer handle the snakes and hold a balloon as the eastern diamondback rattlesnake strikes and pops it. (Scary!) By the way, Florida has four of the six poisonous snakes in the USA. The **Gator Wrestlin' Show** offers a more "educational" and close-up view, where you'll see the trainer flopping around and wrestling (sort of) with an alligator. This is the time to ask questions about reptiles and listen to all kinds answers. Shows are

26

regularly scheduled throughout the day.

The whole thing may sound a little like a tourist trap, but the **cypress swamp walkway** will offer tranquil respite and insight to what Florida may have been like before the tourist invasion. Stroll along the boardwalk through a peaceful swamp leading to the Everglades. For a bird's-eye view of the breeding marsh, climb up into the three-story **observation tower** and gaze around at the activity below.

For a little hands-on action, there's the **petting area** with deer and baby goats. No, there are no gators in the petting area, but there is a baby gator-holding photo opportunity offered nearby. Kids can also sit on Albert, a three hundred-pound tortoise from the Galapagos Islands. Have your cameras ready.

If you're truly adventurous, you might want to try the gator ribs or gator nuggets for lunch. In fact, gator meat has less cholesterol and fat than chicken. I wasn't brave enough to eat the ribs, but the gator nuggets tasted like chicken. (Don't most weird foods?) I *was* brave enough to touch an eighteen-month old alligator, and it felt curiously like a purse or pair of boots.... or is it the other way around?

Age Range: Any age.
Hours: 8:00 A.M. to dusk.
Admission: Adults $10.95, children (3-11) $7.95.
Time Allowance: 3 to 3 1/2 hours.
Directions: (Eastbound on I-4) Take Exit 27A to South Orange Blossom Trail and turn right. It's about 3 miles ahead on the left. (Westbound on I-4) Take Exit 28 on the Beeline Expressway and follow signs for Route 441. Turn right and it's about 6 miles ahead on the left.
Parking: Free.
Wheelchair Accessible: Yes.
Restaurant: Yes, featuring gator ribs and gator nuggets.
Picnicking: Yes.
Rest Rooms: Yes.
Gift Shop: Yes.
Cool Tip: Don't overlook the raised boardwalk through the fifty-acre cypress swamp.

27

HARD ROCK CAFE
5800 Kirkman Road
Orlando, FL 32819
(407) 351-7625

FUN SCALE

It's hip, hot, and happening at The Hard Rock Cafe Orlando. From the parking lot, enter via a walk down the long guitar neck ramp. Stroll into the electric guitar-shaped building delineated in bright neon and encompassing 23,000 square feet next to Universal Studios.

At times the lines are long, but the music is rocking, the employees are entertaining, and people of all ages are having a good time. Pick up a free helium balloon with the Hard Rock Cafe logo on the outside. Enter the building and find a number of things that will blow you away. It's a place to buy really cool T-shirts, pins, and jackets. And it's a burger joint. Look around at all of the rock and roll paraphernalia as you chomp on a "pig sandwich" (pork with famous, vinegar-based barbecue sauce) or slurp down a thick malted milk shake.

Older kids may appreciate Elvis Presley's 1926 Gibson L-5 acoustic guitar or Jimi Hendrix's "Hey Joe" demo record decorating the walls more than the younger kids, but there are other things to interest them. If they're lucky, kids will catch a glimpse of some of the Universal Studios characters.

Oftentimes people like Fred Flintstone, Barney Rubble, Lucy and Desi Arnez, Fivel, or Rocky and Bullwinkle cruise through the cafe. If Jaws had feet, maybe he, too, would stroll through.

Even the rest rooms–with their stall doors stating, "No drugs or nuclear weapons allowed inside"–are cool. The shelves are lined with "useables"–hair gel, cologne, perfume, dental floss, toothpaste, and lip stick, to name a few.

If you're not a rock fan, take ear plugs.

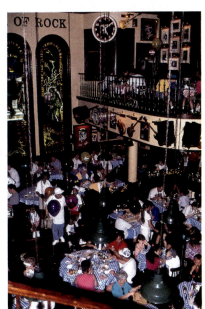

Age Range: Any age. Even the youngest will appreciate all the colors and activity.
Hours: 10:30 A.M. to 2:00 A.M.
Admission: Free.
Time allowance: As long as it takes to walk through or eat a meal and catch some tunes.
Directions: From I-4 take Exit 29 or 30B and follow signs to Universal Studios, which will lead you to signs for Hard Rock Cafe.
Parking: Free.
Wheelchair Accessible: Yes.
Restaurant: Yes.
Picnicking: No.
Rest Rooms: Yes, with changing tables.
Gift Shop: Yes; T-shirts, leather jackets, pins.

KING HENRY'S FEAST
8984 International Drive
Plaza International
Orlando, FL 32819
(407) 363-3500 or (800) 883-8282

FUN SCALE

"Hear ye! Hear ye!" It's His Majesty King Henry VIII's birthday and he's inviting you to a royal celebration. Step back in time to the sixteenth century and experience the gala festivities of a king who's celebrating his birthday *and* looking for his newest bride (the seventh, but who's counting). If you're of the female persuasion and not careful, you may be selected from the audience to be the "chosen one."

It all takes place in a castle constructed from authentic English stone, brick, and timber. There's a moat (minus the gators) surrounding the castle with a wooden draw-bridge. Inside the dining hall you will find enormous wrought-iron chandeliers and heraldic banners hanging from the rafters, long banquet tables, and people dressed in

the regal clothing from the sixteenth century. All set the stage for an evening of feast and festivity.

Sit down and share one of the banquet tables with other guests. The feast starts out with a giant pail of soup followed by salad, chicken and ribs, vegetables and dessert. Wash it down with pitchers of beer, wine, or Coca-Cola. Everything is served in pewter pails and pitchers by "wenches"–young peasant girls. Now's your chance to eat with your hands (if you want to), and shed that restrictive flatware. Go wild! Put on the crown (everyone gets one), roll up your sleeves, and get ready to gorge.

As you search for a way to eat tactfully, without forks and knives, you're

royally entertained by a magician/illusionist who pulls doves from nowhere, by a fire-blowing man who also swallows knives, by a sword fight ending in a draw, and by a trapeze acrobat named Lady Linda. And that names only a few of the entertainments. The show is captivating and well done, and the food plentiful and tasty.

Age Range: 3 to 5 year olds might have trouble sitting for 2 hours. 6 and up are more likely to appreciate the show.
Hours: 7 nights per week. Show times vary with season.
Admission: Adults $31.95, children (3-11) $19.95. Reservations are suggested.
Time Allowance: About 2 hours.
Directions: From I-4 take Exit 29 (Sand Lake Road) and travel south on International Drive. It's on the right
Parking: Free.
Wheelchair Accessible: Yes.
Rest Rooms: Yes.
Gift Shop: No.

MYSTERY FUN HOUSE
5767 Major Boulevard
Orlando, FL 32819
(407) 351-3356

FUN SCALE

Copyright © Mystery Fun House

What can you do on a rainy day, or as an alternative to the larger and more expensive theme parks? Mystery Fun House offers a conglomeration of entertaining activities.

Go into the **Mystery Fun House** and explore fifteen chambers of hidden surprises. Make your way to the *Mirror Maze*. Everywhere you turn you're confronted by mirrors and images of yourself. When you *do* finally escape, follow the sound of the tune "Walk Like an Egyptian" and bop into the *Egyptian Tomb*. You're inside a giant pyramid and challenged by a slanted floor. Look at the mysteriously wrapped mummy behind glass. If you're brave enough, slide down the chute into the *Chamber of Horrors* and see horrible instruments of torture; watch yourself turn into a werewolf. Experience the thrill of walking through a tunnel that spins as you attempt to pass through. Watch that equilibrium!

Should you opt to partake in **Starbase Omega**, you're in for a galactic experience. Suit up with a beltpack. Arm yourself with a laser blaster, and board the starship for the twenty-first century. Land on the alien planet and begin your mission, which is to stay alive. Enter the dark space surrounded by padded and bouncy ground, caves in which to hide, and walls to duck behind, and begin a laser firing frenzy. Just when you think you're safe, a seven-year-old zaps you from behind a boulder. It's you against the other travelers, and you're banking points which will be added up in the end to determine the winner.

Golfers might try **Mystery Mini-Golf**. Aim for a shark's jaw or putt past the wizard's castle gate before it closes. It's a wild and wacky eighteen-hole course. Giant plastic clubs are available for younger children.

Also available is a large **Video Game Room**, and, for the ultimate in thrill seeking, there's **Bungee Jumping**. Prices for each vary, and are not included in the general price of admissions. Call ahead for Bungee Jumping prices and age restrictions.

Age Range: 5 and up. Teenagers love Star Base.
Hours: 10:00 A.M. to 10:00 P.M., daily.
Admission: Mystery Fun House $7.95; Starbase Omega $5.95; Mystery Mini-Golf $2.95; Super Combination $11.85.
Time Allowance: 2 or 3 hours.
Directions: From I-4 take Exit 30B and it's across from Universal Studio's Maingate.
Parking: Free.
Wheelchair Accessible: Yes, all but the "Pit" (the lowest level of the video arcade).
Restaurant: Snackbar only.
Picnicking: Yes, with tables.
Rest Rooms: Yes, with changing tables.
Gift Shop: Yes, T-shirts, sweatshirts, Frisbees.

ORLANDO MUSEUM OF ART
Orlando Loch Haven Park
2416 North Mills Avenue
Orlando, FL 32803
(407) 896-4231

FUN SCALE

Turn your museum visit into a hands-on adventure. The two often don't go together, but the Orlando Art Museum provides both a hands-on *and* museum experience. Disney sponsored **Art Encounters** offers an innovative approach to art education. The exhibits help cultivate a personal understanding of the art and style of other cultures. It also offers a more kid-friendly interpretation of the big people exhibits in the rest of the museum.

Surround yourself with masks, headdresses, and drums in the *West African Room*. Touch certain buttons to activate the computer drums. Piece together the past in the *Archaeology Room*. You'll learn about archaeological digs and find a lightbeam activity teaching about the pre-Columbian Period.

Dress up in the multicultural clothes. Grind some corn on the metate stone (pronounced ma-ta-tay) from Costa Rica. Try a hand on the huge loom and add some layers to the continuous weaving. Return to the USA in the *American Cafeteria*, and experiment with the colorful and textural shapes à la Jim Dine. Fool around with making art on the computer, or flop down into the comfortable bean bag chairs and listen to, or read, a story.

The main part

34

of the museum is worthwhile too. It consists of rotating exhibits as well as a growing collection of ninteenth and twentieth century American art, pre-Columbian artifacts, and African objects. Check out the hands-on exhibit within the **Pre-Columbian Art Gallery** (2000 B.C.-A.D. 1500). Feel the textures of the minerals and gems. Feel the ancient crocodile skin. It won't bite!

Age Range: 3 to 8 will appreciate Art Encounters, and older kids will enjoy the main part of the museum.
Hours: Main galleries open Tuesday through Saturday, 9:00 A.M. to 5:00 P.M.; Sunday from 12:00 noon to 5:00 P.M. Closed Mondays. Art Encounters open Tuesday through Friday and Sunday from 12:00 noon to 5:00 P.M., Saturday from 10:00 A.M. to 5:00 P.M.
Admission: Adults (12 and up) $4.00, children (4-11) $2.00.
Time Allowance: 1 to 2 hours.

Directions: From I-4 take the Princeton exit, and continue east to the park entrance on the left.
Wheelchair Accessible: Yes.
Restaurant: Yes.
Picnicking: Yes.
Rest Rooms: Yes.
Gift Shop: Yes, separate kid's shop too.
Cool Tip: Plan to have a bite to eat in the cafe. The atmosphere is pleasant and the food good.

ORLANDO'S RIPLEY'S BELIEVE IT OR NOT!

**8201 International Drive
Orlando, FL 32819
(407) 363-4418**

FUN SCALE

The outside of Ripley's Believe It or Not! alone is somewhat of an enigma, and it's enough to make you stop and wonder. Is the tilted-building *really* sliding into the earth? Step inside and you're immediately welcomed to the museum by a 3-D hologram projection seated behind the desk. Continue on, and experience even more puzzling and exotic exhibits.

Witness strange animals like the stuffed two-headed kitten, the six-

legged frog, or the two-headed calf. Wonder about the hand-me-down clothes made from human hair. Marvel at the 1907 Rolls Royce built from more than a million matchsticks. Be dwarfed by the sculptures of the tallest (eight-feet-eleven-inches) or the heaviest (half-ton) man. See the **Medieval Torture Chamber** room. Question the human unicorn. Can you roll your tongue? Try it in front of the mirror with the hidden camera, and see yourself looking totally silly on video afterwards.

Step carefully into the forced-perspective room: The pool table's slanted, the floor's slanted, the paintings are slanted, and you, too, are part of the optical illusion. Finally, for the grande finale, a walk down a ramp through the rotating lava tunnel is sure to put you over the edge, or at least to make you dizzy for hours afterward.

Age Range: 6 and up.
Hours: 10:00 A.M. to 11:00 P.M., daily with extended hours during peak season.
Admission: Adults $8.95, children (4-11) $5.95.
Time Allowance: About an hour.
Directions: From I-4 take Exit 29 for Sand Lake Road. Travel east on Sand Lake Road and turn right (southbound) on International Drive. Ripley's is ahead on your left.
Parking: Free.
Wheelchair Accessible: Yes.
Restaurant: No.
Picnicking: No.
Rest Rooms: Yes.
Gift Shop: Yes; T-shirts, posters, games.

ORLANDO SCIENCE CENTER
810 East Rollins Street
Orlando, FL 32803
(407) 896-7151

FUN SCALE

Copyright © Orlando Science Center

Crash! Zap! Bolts of lightning... Have you ever had the urge to create a tornado? How about to surround yourself in a bubble, or trade your tired old scallop shell in for a dazzling new whelk egg case? All this and more can be done at the Orlando Science Center.

Aside from some dazzling and exciting changing shows, there are ultra-cool permanent exhibits. For instance, in **Natureworks** you'll come face-to-face with a real-live alligator and be able to leaf through the extensive collection of shells, bones, and fossils. This is the place to swap your most cherished natural object for another even more cherished object. The **Trading Center** system works in a way that, the more you know about your item, the more trading points it's worth. "Bank" your points toward one special item. The more you know, the more you get.

Step into the **Tunnel of Discovery**, and unlock the doors to the playground in your mind. Experiment with various activities dealing in optical illusion and gravity. Look at the world from inside a giant bubble. Unravel some of the mysteries of physical science.

Copyright © Orlando Science Center

Waterworks is a kid's playspace designed for mini-scientists, age three to seven. Learn about the principles of water by piloting a huge rubber raft. Act out plays in the **Water Life Puppet Theatre,** and see yourself on the TV screen. Climb under the turtle display, look up through the glass, and see how things might look from a turtle's perspective.

Copyright © Orlando Science Center

Experience the wonders of the universe in the **John Young Planetarium**. Have a seat in the round room, and relax as outer space unfolds right before your eyes. Focus on planets, constellations, and other celestial objects of the current night sky. Stay tuned for the nighttime **Cosmic Concerts**, and encounter **laser shows** to the beat of rock'n'roll. Call for show information.

Finally, predict and analyze the weather through **Weather Central**. Track hurricanes or, at the touch of a button, check out the atmospheric conditions around the world.

Age Range: The "targeted" age range is from 4 to 11, but both older and younger viewers will also enjoy the experience.
Hours: Monday through Thursday and Saturday from 9:00 A.M. to 5:00 P.M., Friday from 9:00 A.M. to 9:00 P.M., Sunday from 12:00 noon to 5:00 P.M. Closed Christmas and Thanksgiving.
Admission: Adults $6.50, children (3-11) $5.50. Planetarium Show included.
Time Allowance: 2 to 4 hours.
Directions: From I-4 take Exit 43 and proceed east for 1/4 mile on Princeton Street. Turn left into Loch Haven Park.
Parking: Free.
Wheelchair Accessible: Yes.
Restaurant: Snackbar only.
Picnicking: Yes.
Rest Rooms: Yes, with changing tables.
Gift Shop: Yes; cool crawly things, T-shirts, science kits.

39

SEA WORLD

7007 Sea World Drive
Orlando, FL 32821
(407) 351-3600

FUN SCALE

A day at Sea World means a day of exploration and learning through exposure to everything marine, including penguins galore, a myriad of manatees, and a breathtaking killer-whale exhibit. Select those attractions which interest you, and immerse yourself in the world of the sea. Here are some shows and exhibits you might particularly like.

In **Shamu: New Visions**, an upbeat narrated presentation, experience an up-close encounter with both Shamu (Mama) and Baby Shamu as these cetaceans swim and splash together in the water. **Bermuda Triangle** offers a one-of-a-kind experience. The simulated ride takes you a mile along the edge of the trench to find out what lurks below. Heed the health restrictions written at the entrance. It's fairly demanding, physically and mentally, and may be too much for the little people.

Back on the surface, check out **Hotel Clyde & Seamore**. See walruses, a team of otters, and a sea lion duo perform hilariously, acting out a skit which includes an evil woman trying to ruin the hotel's rating and an aerobics class being instructed by a huge walrus. Imagine that! Walk through the glass tunnel into **Terrors of the Deep** and surround yourself with a terrifying collection of dangerous sea creatures, including eels, sharks and barracuda. The eerie music in the background adds to the tone of the experience, which is one of

Sea World's most exciting.

The **Pacific Point Preserve** sets the scene for sea lions, and both harbor and fur seals, all of which have webbed front flippers. Listen to the vocal seals barking about something or other, as they interact with each other and dive in and out of the water. Through the living laboratory glass of **Penguin Encounter**, watch the curious birds generally stand statue-like and, occasionally, waddle over to the edge and dive into the water. The display is designed in such a way that you see them both in and out of the water. Catch the water-eye view from the moving walkway.

In **Manatees: The Last Generation?** immerse yourself in the world of a fascinating endangered Florida creature. Explore the underwater world of the gentle giants and watch them swim around in the three-and-a-half acre habitat.

Learn about ways in which we can help prevent their extinction. Man is their main threat and, as the sign states, "Extinction is forever. Endangered means we still have time..."

Have you ever touched a stingray? In **Stingray Lagoon** you have the chance. They only sting, it turns out, when they're stepped on. The narrator talks about how to avoid the sting by doing the "stingray shuffle," while walking through waters that might be infested with the slimy creatures. They're cool to

touch as they swim by. Lean over and try!

Shamu's Happy Harbor offers a little respite for the younger children. It's a four-story, three-acre playspace with crawlable, climbable, explorable places in a nautical style where they can burn-off extra energy.

Age Range: Any age will find entertainment. There are interactive/hands-on dolphin and stingray pools for the little people and a zillion other things for the bigger ones.

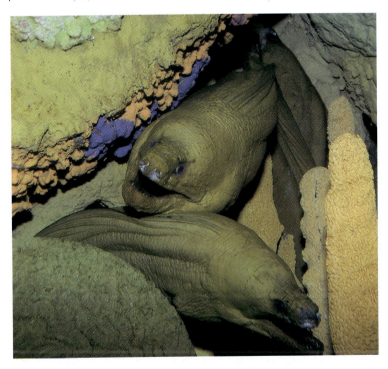

Hours: Open year-round from 9:00 A.M. to 7:00 P.M. Hours vary during summer and on holidays.
Admission: Adults (10 and up) $34.95, Children (3-9) $29.95. *Two-day pass*: Adults $39.95, Children $34.95. Strollers, wheelchairs, and lockers available for rental. Free kennels for pets.
Time allowance: About 8 hours.
Directions: Take the Beeline Expressway exit off I-4. Follow the signs and you're there.
Parking: $5 per day.
Wheelchair Accessible: Yes, in most places.
Restaurant: Yes.
Picnicking: No.
Rest Rooms: Yes, with changing tables.
Gift Shop: Yes; stuffed whales, posters, T-shirts.
Cool Tip: I would suggest doing the "Bermuda Triangle" in the early morning or late afternoon to avoid long lines. As for the shows like "Shamu: New Visions," get there twenty minutes early to get a good seat. By the way, the front row isn't necessarily the best seat–unless you really want to get wet.

SPLENDID CHINA
3000 Splendid China Boulevard
Kissimmee, FL 34747
(407) 397-8800

FUN SCALE

The audience here is generally older, but if you need a "time out" from the simulation-overload of Orlando theme parks and want a taste of the Orient, a day at Splendid China might be just the answer. It's also a place to learn about the fascinating history of China. The newly opened cultural attraction has captivating performance art and carefully recreated, hand-made exhibits that represent the five thousand year history and ten thousand square miles of China.

Begin the journey by looking over the free map, and selecting sites and performances which most interest you. There are numerous sites on seventy-six acres to explore. Make sure to work some of the scheduled live entertainment (from acrobatics to knife climbing) into your itinerary.

Head to **Suzhou Gardens** and experience a full-sized Chinese main street, circa A.D. 1300, complete with shopping, dining, and displays on the diversity of Chinese culture.

Dominating the landscape is **The Great Wall**, which winds along the park for more than half a mile. The original Great Wall spans 4,200 miles and is visible to astronauts from space. Splendid China's Great Wall was constructed from over six million, two-inch long bricks, and was painstakingly laid, brick by brick, by Chinese artisans.

You can't miss **The Lunan Stone Forest**; its towering limestone peaks create the park's centerpiece. The original, massive formations in China were literally carved by nature over the millennia into beautiful and wild configurations.

Don't miss the underground **terra cotta warrior figures**. The story has it that, in 1974, a farmer was out in the field digging a well when he came across eight thousand life-sized soldiers, horses, and fighting vehicles made of clay. Imagine coming across such a find! The figures have been recreated–life-sized–and can be seen in their underground digs.

If the younger children need an energy outlet, take them to **Panda Playground**. It's a play area with climbing nets, slides, sand, and bounce spaces.

Don't miss the thirty-five foot, hand-carved replica statue of the **Leshan Grand Buddha**. Although not as large as the twenty-four story high original, it's awesome nonetheless.

Another "not to miss" is **Imperial Palace**, a replica from the Forbidden City. The mini-version with six thousand rooms has been reproduced stone by stone, tile by tile, and brush stroke by minute brush stroke.

Sample the authentic Chinese cuisine. The assortment of eateries offer eaters a variety of dishes from **Cantonese** to **Szechuan** to **Hunan**, and are worth a stop on your journey. My eggroll was the best I've ever eaten!

Age Range: Kids 3 to 8 will have a difficult time unless with enthusiastic parents; other than the play area in the Panda Playground, there's not much that's hands-on. Kids 9 to 12 will appreciate the performances and exhibits, and might appreciate the historical information.

Hours: *Park*–9:30 A.M. to 8:00 P.M., daily. *Restaurants*–9:30 A.M. to 9:30 P.M.

Admission: Adults (13 and up) $23.00, Children (5 to 12) $13.90, Military $20.00, Seniors $21.90.

Time Allowance: 5 to 7 hours if planning to eat a meal.

Directions: Take Exit 25B off of I-4 and travel west on Rt. 192 for 2 miles. It's on your left.

Parking: Free.

Wheelchair Accessible: Yes.

Restaurant: Yes, from fine dining to casual snacking.

Picnicking: No.

Rest Rooms: Yes.

Gift Shop: Yes; chopsticks, dolls, hats, scattered throughout the park.

UNIVERSAL STUDIOS
1000 Universal Studios Plaza
Orlando, FL 32819
(407) 363-8000

FUN SCALE

This is the "number 1 movie studio and theme park in the world," and with good reason. The 444-acre, studio backlot includes such greats as Jaws, the thirty-two foot, three-ton killer shark; Kongfrontation, the six-ton ape; and the E.T. Adventure. As you soar through the sky on the back of E.T.'s bicycle, crashing through the city streets of King Kong's kingdom, and cruising through the shark-infested waters, there's a fine line between fantasy and reality.

Before venturing any further into the world where boundaries between illusion and reality are lowered, sit down and chart your course. When lines are longer in the summer, strategy is the key. Plan to do the more popular rides–Jaws, Hanna-Barbara, E.T., Back to the Future, Earthquake, and Kongfrontation–either early in the morning or late in the afternoon when the lines are shorter.

You might begin your day by with a stroll down Fifth Avenue past Central Park. Check out the Guggenheim Museum! It's a "forced perspective"

technique where two-dimensional cut-outs appear three-dimensional. It's a technique that Alfred Hitchcock used in his films. If you're brave enough, step into **Kongfrontation** for a confrontation with King Kong–all 13,000 pounds and thirty-five angry feet of him. You're taken, via cable car, through Manhattan as the escaped gorilla stalks you. Trains crash, ambulances roll, buildings burst into flames, and you're left dangling over the East River. Hold on to the kids!

Earthquake rates an *8.3* on the Richter Scale, which means *ten* on the Fun Scale. You're in a subway careening through the city streets surrounded by major water leaks, streets crumbling, trucks sliding, trains crashing, and buildings bursting into flame. It's heart-poundingly scary, and almost too real.

For a pleasant "time out," pick up a special boarding pass and hop aboard the starbound bicycle with E.T. as your guide. Travel through outer space past aliens, stars, and planets in the **E.T. Adventure.** At the end of the journey listen for E.T. to say your name. It's a wonderful experience and a favorite among kids.

A short cruise on the outdoor boatride might be just the key to returning to earth. Board the boat for a ride through shark-infested waters. Not just any shark, but a thirty-two foot, three-ton killer appropriately named **Jaws**. You're unexpectedly cruising along when, all of a sudden, the monster bursts out of the water through flames and explosions. "Nothing can stop him."

Enter the world of **Hanna-Barbara**. Feel what it would be like inside a cartoon as you speed through Bedrock and familiarize yourself with Yogi Bear, The Flintstones, Elroy Jetson, and others. It's interactive, it's fast, and it's fun!

Although **Back to the Future... The Ride** may sound somewhat tame,

it's anything but. Heed the height (forty-inch minimum) and health restrictions posted at the entry. Climb into the space ship and travel through an Ice-Age encounter with dinosaurs, falling rocks, and an erupting volcano. Travel, at the speed of light, through a valley. It's a physically jarring and startling experience. You might want not want to eat lunch until afterwards.

Hitchcock's 3-D Theatre may not be the most fun attraction for the kids, but the older audience will find it entertaining. It's "in-your-face" horror–Alfred Hitchcock style. Reenact the memorable shower scene in *Psycho*. Feel the feathered friends as they attack you in a scene from *The Birds*. Learn some of the secrets behind Hitchcock's masterpieces.

Who ya gonna call when the ghosts are out of control? Ghostbusters, of course. In **Ghostbusters Spectacular**, another spookily-themed attraction, but more geared toward kids, transform yourself into one. Suit up, grab a ghost trap, and fire your Nutrana Wand. The cast includes fourteen larger-than-life ghosts, and the set is haunted. You never know who may drop in for a visit.

If you're between five and twelve, and like slime-erupting geysers, learning all about gak, and peeking behind the scenes in a TV studio, then a visit to the **Nickelodeon Studio** is a must. Volunteer to test some of the new games that may be used on Nickelodeon shows. Spin through Production Alley and get a close look at wardrobe and make-up. Check out the Gak Meister's kitchen and see how gak and slime are made. Speaking of slime, you may just have a chance to "get slimed" during a demonstration!

Animal Actors is a live performance of your favorite cuddly friends. Remember Lassie? A talking horse named Mr. Ed? A big fluffy dog named Beethoven? All are here doing spectacular and comical maneuvers.

If your kids are six or younger, plan to spend some time in **Fievel's Playland.** No lines, no simulation, just plain old fun. Experience things from a mouse's point of view. Jump around inside a one thousand-gallon cowboy hat. Climb a giant spider

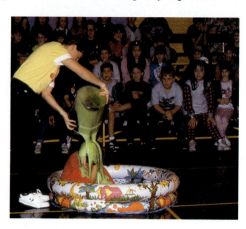

web. Ride a raft down the rapids of a wild water slide–expect to get wet!

Wanting to leave space for other places in this guide book, I've only mentioned *some* of the exciting attractions at Universal Studios. There are plenty of others to explore.

Age Range: Be forewarned that a lot of what's here is for older kids and may be too scary for the little ones. The attractions rated "PG" (Jaws, Kongfrontation, Back to the Future, Hitchcock's 3-D Theatre, Earthquake, and the Horror Make-up Show) are too demanding for some children. There *are* shows geared specially for young kids (Nickelodeon Studios Tour, Animal Actors Show, E.T. Adventure, and Fievel's Playland), and adults will enjoy them too.

Hours: *Winter*— 9:00 A.M. to 7:00 P.M., daily. *Summer*–9:00 A.M. to 11:00 P.M., daily.

Admission: *One-Day Ticket*–Adults (10 and up) $35.00, children (3-9) $28.00. *Two-Day Ticket*–Adults (10 and up) $55.00, children (3-9) $44.00. Jurassic Park strollers available for $5.00 per day.

Time Allowance: *Winter*—allow a full day. *Summer*–allow for 1 1/2 to 2 days due to lines.

Directions: From I-4 take Exit 29 (Sand Lake Road) and follow the signs.

Parking: $5.00 per day, $11.00 valet per day.

Wheelchair Accessible: Yes.

Restaurant: Yes, many.

Picnicking: Yes, in Central Park.

Rest Rooms: Yes, with changing tables.

Gift Shop: Yes, at practically every corner.

Cool Tip: If you're with another adult and your small children can't go on some of the rides, try *"Baby Swap."* Go to the handicap entrance of any ride and tell the attendant that you want to do the "Baby Swap." One adult would then go on the ride, while the other waited with the children. When s/he returns, they swap and the other enters the ride–free of any line waiting.

WATER MANIA

6073 West Irlo Bronson Highway (U.S. 192)
Kissimmee, FL 34746
(407) 396-2626

FUN SCALE

Copyright © David Woods

A nice combination of simulated water rides–from relaxing to down-right terrifying–mixed with the pastoral setting of a picnic area distinguish this park. Thirty-six acres of these water rides, along with volleyball courts, a pastoral picnic setting and a kiddie play area, allow for a variety of excitement.

You don't have to be a surfer to appreciate **Wipe-out**. Grab a boogie board and ride the waves (or they'll ride you) on this fast-moving, appropriately named ride. Or, should you opt to ride **The Abyss**, you'll be enclosed in a tube and shoot twisting and turning through over three hundred feet of deep-blue darkness before reaching the end. Other rides include an exciting whitewater adventure in a tube on **Riptide**.

For more kid-oriented activity, explore the **Rain Forest**–a kiddie pool featuring slides, climbable giant turtles, fountains, and a new **Pirate Ship**. Climb aboard and play with the water slides, spraying treasure chest, tunnels, and cannons. Kids spend all day pretending to be pirates. They also can wade around in the **Squirt Pond**, which includes a sandy beach surrounded by huge umbrellas and chairs so parents can catch some rays or relax.

Age Range: Any age.
Hours: Vary from month to month. Call for hours.
Admission: Adult (13 and older) $19.95, children (3-12) $17.95. Tube and locker rentals available.
Time Allowance: 3 hours to full day.
Directions: From I-4 take Exit 25A and head east for 1 mile. It's on the left.
Parking: $2.00.
Wheelchair Accessible: Around rides only.
Restaurant: Snackbar only.
Picnicking: Yes, barbecue pits and grills provided.
Rest Rooms: Yes, with showers and changing tables.
Gift Shop: Yes.

WET 'N WILD
6200 International Drive
Orlando, FL 32819
(407) 351-1800 or (800) 992-WILD

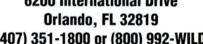

FUN SCALE

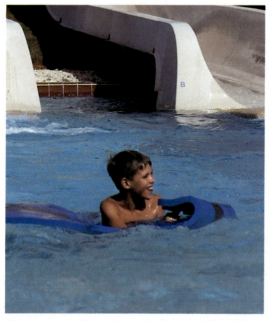

Is the hot weather getting you down? Are you suffering from the lack-of-momentum blues? Are you in need of a wild wake-up? If so, a day at Wet 'n Wild might be just the cure.

It's a water park with eye-opening rides of all kinds. For tubing options, you have a choice between rides like **Raging Rapids**, where you'll tube through white waters and whirlpools on your way to the final waterfall plunge, and **The Surge**, where you and four other passengers will tube down five stories through almost six hundred feet of twisting, turning curves.

Super slide rides offer a different sort of thrill–the "free-fall." The **Mach 5** offers a choice of five different flumes totaling 2,500 feet which, twisting and turning, end in an abrupt splash. **Der Stuka**, the six-story speed slide, allows you to free-fall down a 250-foot slide, coming to a gliding stop along a 115-foot long waterway. Awesome!

The **Kid's Playground**, for those under forty-eight inches, lets children splash around on mini-versions of the adult rides. Adults must accompany the kids.

For the less brave, other options include the giant **Surf Lagoon**, an ocean-like wave pool simulation alternating between turbulent and calm, and **Knee Ski**, a half-mile long kneeboard course around a lake. By the way, there are lifeguards at each site and the water is kept at a comfortable temperature year round.

Age Range: Any age, if you're a water lover.
Hours: Open daily, but hours change monthly. Call for schedule.
Admission: Adults (10 and up) $20.95, children (3-9) $17.95. *Second Day Pass*–$10.45. *Optional Rentals*–Tubes: $4.00 plus $1.00 deposit. Towels: $1.00. Lockers: $3.00 plus $2.00 deposit. Life Vests: $1.00.
Time Allowance: 3 hours to a full day.
Directions: From I-4 take Exit 30A and head south on International Drive. It's ahead on the left.
Parking: Free.
Wheelchair Accessible: Around the rides only.
Restaurant: Yes.
Picnicking: Yes, but no glassware or alcoholic beverages.
Rest Rooms: Yes, with showers.
Gift Shop: Yes; T-shirts, bathing suits, towels, sunglasses.

WILD BILL'S WILD WEST DINNER EXTRAVAGANZA

5260 U.S. 192 (East of I-4)
Kissimmee, FL 34746
(407) 363-3500 or (800) 883-8282

FUN SCALE

Situated in an authentic western fort and happening during the American centennial, Wild Bill's Wild West Dinner Extravaganza comes to life for two hours of gut-busting and side-splitting food and fun.

Step back into the year 1876 and enter the days of wagon trains, cavalry troops, and dance hall saloons. You're in for a two-hour hoe-down hosted by Wild Bill and Miss Kitty who take you through a number of rip-roaring performances, including a storytelling session, cowboy antics, and a knife-throwing and arrow-shooting demonstration.

Native American Commanche Indians dressed in authentic feather headdresses and costumes make the scene colorful. They put on a spectacular tribal dance performance.

It's all happening as you chomp on a feast consisting of soup, salad, fried chicken, barbecued ribs, corn-on-the-cob, baked potato, and apple pie. Also included are beer, wine, and Coca Cola. You can also see the life-like tableaus in the **Brave Warrior Wax Museum**, which depicts the beauty of the untamed west.

Age Range: Kids 3 to 5 might have trouble sitting for two hours; 6 and up are more likely to appreciate the show.
Hours: Two shows daily from 7:00 to 9:00 P.M. and 9:00 to 11:00 P.M. Show times vary with season. Reservations are suggested.
Admission: *Dinner Show*–adults $31.95, children (3-11) $19.95.
Brave Warrior Wax Museum–adults $4.00, children (3-11) $2.00.
50% discount to the museum for those attending the dinner show.
Time Allowance: Shows last for 2 hours.
Directions: From I-4 take the Exit 25 and travel east on U.S. 192. It's ahead on your right.
Parking: Free.
Wheelchair Accessible: Yes.
Restaurant: Yes.
Picnicking: No.
Rest Rooms: Yes.
Gift Shop: Yes; coonskin caps, moccasins, Civil War memorabilia.

GREEN MEADOWS PETTING FARM
P.O. Box 420787
Kissimmee, FL 34742
(407) 846-0770

FUN SCALE

Copyright © Green Meadows

For a change of pace from bustling Orlando, choose a nice day and take a drive out to the Green Meadows Petting Farm. Cool groves of live oaks bearded with Spanish moss provide the environment for the farm. Ostriches, ducks, pot-bellied pigs, free-roaming peacocks, donkeys, and an American bison, provide the entertainment.

Take a tour and learn about farm animals through first-hand experiences. Reach out and pet a pig, stroke a sheep, or even milk a cow. Jump on a tractor wagon and experience a *real* hayride. Take a guided ride on the back of a pony. Check out the silly green eggs–they're from a South American chicken.

Age Range: Any age up to 12. Teens might not find it too exciting. Adults will appreciate their children's interest.
Hours: 9:30 A.M. to 5:30 P.M., daily. Tours begin at 9:30 A.M. and go continuously until 4:00 P.M. Closed on Christmas and Thanksgiving.
Admission: $12.00 per person. Children (under 2) free.
Time Allowance: 2 to 4 hours.
Directions: From I-4 take Exit 25A and go east on Route 192 for 3 miles. Turn right at Poinciana Boulevard. It's 5 miles ahead on your right.
Parking: Free.
Wheelchair Accessible: Yes.
Restaurant: Snackbar only.
Picnicking: Yes, with barbecues and tables.
Rest Rooms: Yes, with a communal changing table.
Gift Shop: Yes.

CYPRESS GARDENS
P.O. Box 1
Cypress Gardens, FL 33884
(813) 324-2111

FUN SCALE

It's a magical botanical wonderland. Excite your senses with a visual and aromatic overload. Cypress Gardens is located on two hundred acres of lush gardens and towering cypress trees. It's a place to witness fluttering butterflies, water-skiers, acrobats, and blooming botanical displays.

A favorite of mine was the **Wings of Wonder** display. Picture yourself in a glass-enclosed atrium. You're surrounded by tropical plants, mini-waterfalls are rushing by, and classical music is playing in the background. There are butterflies galore and they're fluttering all around you. Iguanas are hiding in the banana leaves, and turtles are splashing about in the water. It's a glorious experience!

A note on acclimatizing for Wings of Wonder–it's almost overwhelmingly hot and humid. Eyeglasses and camera lenses initially fog up; you might want to spend a few minutes allowing for your glasses (and your body) to adjust.

Long recognized as the "water-ski capitol of the world," Cypress Gardens has grown famous for its astonishing aquatic presentations. Costumed performers execute fascinating stunts including 360-degree maneuvers, hot dogging, and four-tier human pyramids. Check out the barefoot antics of septuagenarian "Banana George" Blair, a crowd favorite for years. **Water-Ski Shows** are regularly scheduled throughout the day.

For an overview of the park, hop on **Kodak's Island in the Sky**. Get a 360-degree view as the revolving platform takes you 153 feet in the air. The trip takes ten minutes and runs every ten minutes.

Train fans will enjoy **Cypress Junction**. Take a self-guided tour through a miniature train village. See the trains travel through different parts of the world. Creative use of smoke and other special effects make this a fascinating display–a definite "not to be missed."

Children under six will be magnetized to **Carousel Cove.** This amusement ride area features eight rides, ranging from a mini-motor boat to an antique-replica carousel.

Live entertainment can be seen at different times throughout the gardens. **Feathered Follies** features a colorful cast of performing birds combining entertainment with fun. See macaws, cockatoos, and Amazon parrots perform captivating stunts right before your eyes! There is a **live production** that features acrobatics and daredevil stunts, and changes biannually.

Take an **Electric Boat Ride** down "Palm Lane." Enjoy a quiet journey through a maze of winding canals that take you past bougainvillea bushes, hibiscus flowers, twenty-seven varieties of palm trees, and live "Southern Belles" decorating the shores.

Age Range: Kids 2 to 5 enjoy the rides. Teenagers appreciate the Water Skiing Demonstration. Everyone loves Wings of Wonder. There's something of interest for all.

Hours: 9:30 A.M. to 5:30 P.M., 365 days of the year.

Admission: Adults $24.95, seniors $21.95, children (3-9) $16.45. Pet facility available; price based on cage size.

Time Allowance: About 5 hours.

Directions: From I-4 take I-27 south to Rt. 540 West.

Parking: Free.

Wheelchair Accessible: Yes.

Restaurant: Yes, and snackbars.

Picnicking: Yes; tables are outside the park.

Rest Rooms: Yes, with changing tables in most rest rooms.

Gift Shop: Yes; sweatshirts, dried butterflies, stationery.

Cool Tip: Save one of the live shows for last. It's a welcome break after a long day of walking.

Copyright © Cypress Gardens

CLEARWATER MARINE SCIENCE CENTER

249 Windward Passage
Clearwater, FL 34630
(813) 441-1790

FUN SCALE

Other than the slippery sea creatures, there's nothing actually slick about Clearwater Marine Science Center (C.M.S.C). There are no computer laser fish games, no cellular dinosaurs, no simulated ocean dives–just a very real environment of ocean creatures and the results of the hard work of more than one hundred caring volunteers. Along with coastal research, rescue and rehabilitation of sea mammals is carried out here.

C.M.S.C. is known for its **turtle research**. The turtles have been rescued and are being rehabilitated. Some are released back into the wild, while others

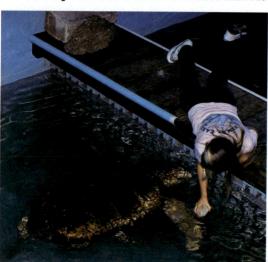

remain permanent residents. "Slick," a young green sea turtle, was found in the Gulf of Mexico covered with dark slime from an oil spill. He's being treated and, after rehabilitation, will be released into the ocean. Check out "Moe," the loggerhead turtle. His weight vacillates between 320 and 400 pounds. In captivity a turtle can live from fifty to one hundred years.

The **Mangrove Seagrass Tank** holds 55,000 gallons of water with mangrove trees, seagrasses, 100 species of fish, and invertebrates inside. Get a close-up view through the glass, which magnifies what you see, of a typical Florida estuary. Walk upstairs and look down from above. You'll be surprised to see how much smaller everything really is.

Dolphins are a big part of C.M.S.C.'s efforts. They're often found dehydrated and stranded, and, after a great deal of rehabilitation, are re-released into the ocean environment. **Dolphin Demonstrations** are given regularly throughout the day. See "Sunset Sam," the Atlantic bottlenose

dolphin, do tricks for fish rewards–he jumps, he talks, he even paints on a canvas. "Sunset Sam" is a permanent resident due to his visual impairment and liver condition.

Don't miss the other exhibits. There's a small **Touch Tank** with shells and starfish. See the **Shell Display** that's organized by the Sun Coast Conchologists. Peek in at the **sea horse** and tiny **pinfish** display. An interesting fact about sea horses is the babies are borne by Papa starfish! Mama starfish lays the eggs in Papa's pouch and splits. (Not bad, eh?) By the way, starfish eat those tiny little pinfish that you see swimming around.

Age Range: Any age.
Hours: Monday through Friday 9:00 A.M. to 5:00 P.M., Saturday 9:00 A.M. to 4:00 P.M., Sunday 11:00 A.M. to 4:00 P.M.
Admission: Adults $4.25, children (3-11) $2.75.
Time Allowance: 1 to 2 hours.
Directions: Take S.R. 60 west almost to the end and follow the signs.
Parking: Free.
Wheelchair Accessible: Yes.
Restaurant: No.
Picnicking: Yes.
Rest Rooms: Yes.
Gift Shop: Yes; shark's teeth, T-shirts, paintings done by dolphins.

ADVENTURE ISLAND
P.O. Box 9158
Tampa, FL 33674
(813) 987-5660

FUN SCALE

Looking for refreshing fun? A lazy, peaceful float down a river? A heart-stopping, seven-story, free-fall drop down a seventy-six foot body slide? Then spending the day at Busch Garden's Adventure Island, the thirty-six acre outdoor water theme park, is the way to go.

Begin with **Aruba Tuba**, the newest water attraction in the park. Experience the "totally tubular" slide as you wind, twist, and turn–at startling speeds.

Fabian's Funport is an area devoted to youngsters (with parents nearby). The scaled-down wave pool allows children to play in the jumping jets and bubbler springs. Climb **Volcano Mountain** and slide down one of the two chutes into the pool area below. Splash!

In the **Rambling Bayou** you'll float down a river on giant inner tube, and pass under bridges, around curves, and through a simulated rain forest. You'll drift at a comfortable pace through weather ranging from mist to a monsoon.

Should you choose

62

to partake in the **Tampa Typhoon**, you'll encounter an exciting free-fall b
slide, dropping from the height of seventy-six feet. Fear not–the ride ends b
leveling off on a flat sliding water trough, not a brick wall.

For a relaxing regular-old (well, almost) swimming experience, you might
opt to go to **Paradise Lagoon**. The nine thousand square-foot pool, fed by
cascading waterfalls and built into cliffs, has diving platforms, a cannonball
slide, and translucent tube slides. Climb across the hand-over-hand rope walk
stretching overhead. You might just think you're on "Gilligan's Island."

If water isn't your bag, or you just need a "time out," check out the **Spike
Zone**. It's a professional quality, twelve-court volleyball area, featuring fine
white sand and lights for night playing.

Age Range: 3 and up.
Hours: March 19 through September 6, and weekends only September 11 through October 24,
10:00 a.m. to 5:00 p.m., daily, with hours extended during summer and selected holiday periods.
Admission: Adults $16.95, children (3-9) $14.95. Children 8 and under must have adult
supervision.
Time Allowance: 3 hours to full day.
Directions: Coming from Orlando westbound on I-4, exit north on I-75. From I-75 take the Fowler
Avenue (Exit 54), and follow signs. From Tampa on I-275, take the Busch Boulevard (Exit 33) and
follow the signs.
Parking: Free.
Wheelchair Accessible: Around the rides only.
Restaurant: Yes, cafes.
Picnicking: Yes.
Rest Rooms: Yes, with showers.
Gift Shop: Yes; bathing suits, towels, T-shirts.

Copyright © Adventure Island

TAMPA

BUSCH GARDENS
P.O. Box 9158
Tampa, FL 33674
(813) 987-5171

FUN SCALE

Have you ever been face to face with a gorilla, felt your stomach leave you as you plunge into a loop at 60 mph on the roller-coaster-record-breaking Kumba ride, seen exotic belly dancers performing in a Moroccan Palace

Copyright © Bush Gardens, Tampa, FL

Theatre, or gotten wet on a raft cruising down the Congo River? It can be done, and all in the same day, at the African-themed Busch Gardens.

There are a number of ways to "do" Busch Gardens. You might start with a twenty-minute **Trans-Veldt Railway** ride through the Serengeti Plain and circumnavigate the park. You have the option to jump off at certain stops or continue through the entire ride. It's a good way to get an overview of the park, and you'll pass ibex, ostriches, zebras, and monkeys among other creatures. Another option for getting an overview is to hop on the **monorail** or the **skyride** to get a view from above. Or, there's always foot power. Hoof around on your own two feet and get face to face with the animals.

You need to hop on the monorail, the train, or the skyride to experience the **Serengeti Plain**, and it's worth it. Explore the "Dark Continent" and see hundreds of African animals roaming freely on the grassy savanna. Lions, gazelles, zebras, rhinoceros, and many others stomp, slither, swim, and siesta out in the open.

You can see the chimps just hanging out or sitting "Thinker" style on the rocks in **Nairobi** at the *Myombe Reserve:The Great Ape Domain.* Get face to face (okay, you're separated by a piece of glass) with our hairy cousins, and check out the curious interactions between chimps and gorillas. The younger kids may enjoy the *petting zoo.* Reach out and touch those goats, sheep, pigs,

turtles, and chickens. Explore the *Nairobi Animal Nursery* and see assorted baby animals that have been injured being cared for. Aren't the ducklings cute?

In **Morocco** you'll step into a bustling city of craft demonstrations, snake charmers, leather smells, metal smiths pounding away on jewelry, restaurants, and theatre entertainment. It's much like real Morocco, minus obnoxious hustlers and vendors. And don't expect to bargain for any souvenirs. You'll find heart-stopping rides in the **Congo**, if you're into that sort of thing; and even if you haven't *been*, you may *be* after a visit to Busch Gardens. Shoot the rapids in the raft on the *Congo River Rapids*, and get set to get wet. The most spectacular, and also the newest, ride is *Kumba*. Experience three minutes of sheer terror and intense fear while riding on the fastest (60 mph) and largest steel rollercoaster in the southeast. You'll encounter the world's largest vertical loop, a diving stunt plane maneuver, and a 360-degree spiraling comeback. Yikes! I, not a huge amusement ride enthusiast, left shaking and dizzy, but with a huge smile on my face. Oh, and don't miss the startlingly beautiful white and yellow Bengal tigers on *Claw Island*, an oasis-like habitat.

Stanleyville, the African-style village, explodes with the excitement of the *Tanganyika Tidal Wave* ride which lulls riders

through a tranquil jungle journey and then plunges them over a waterfall, landing fifty-five feet below into a lagoon. There's also live entertainment and a shopping bazaar.

Kids under six will enjoy *Dwarf Village* in **Bird Gardens**. It's an area where they can ride a carousel, a Model T car, a mini-train, or a boat shaped like a log. Beware–height restrictions apply. Try your arm at throwing softballs in the Ball Cage or jump around in the Soft Bounce Cage. Go into the Playhouse and slide down the slide or climb around on the nets. Dwarf Village is also an area where *The Littlest Zebra Show* takes place. Kids sit on toadstools, watch, and take part in the performance in which they may be asked

to come up and put on a crazy elephant mask. The cute performance lasts about fifteen minutes and is regularly scheduled throughout the day.

You should also check out the *World of Birds Show*, which runs at scheduled times throughout the day and can be a welcome thirty minutes of sitting and being entertained. Where else will you find a laughing and talking parrot named Lolita singing "Oh What a Beautiful Morning?" Or Fifi, the Military macaw from the rain forest, taking a dollar bill right out of an unsuspecting person's hand in the audience? The park is dedicated to saving the rain forest; a talk that is both educational and fun is given on our part in the life cycle of the rain forest and how we affect its future.

Age Range: 3 and up. There's something for everyone, but some rides are more appropriate for certain ages than others.
Hours: 9:30 a.m. to 6 p.m., daily, except summer and selected holiday periods when hours are extended.
Admission: Adults $29.95, kids (3-9) $23.95.
Time allowance: Full day.
Directions: Coming from Orlando westbound on I-4, exit north on I-75. From I-75 take Fowler Avenue (Exit 54), and follow the signs. From Tampa northbound on I-275, take Busch Boulevard (Exit 33), and follow the signs.
Parking: $3.00 per car.
Wheelchair Accessible: Yes.
Restaurants: Yes.
Picnicking: No.
Rest rooms: Yes, with changing tables.
Gift Shop: Yes, many.
Cool Tip: During peak times (summer and holidays), visit the newest, most popular rides (like Kumba) either early in the morning or before closing to avoid long lines.

LOWRY PARK ZOO
7530 North Boulevard
Tampa, FL 33604
(813) 935-8552

FUN SCALE

Come face to face with rare species from all over the world in a natural environment. Watch pygmy marmosets swing through the trees, Sumatran tigers do their elaborate courtship dance, and Florida manatees chomp on lettuce heads. It's a zoo dedicated to preserving the life and dignity of all animals, while continuing to explore the age-old bond between man and beast.

The zoo's natural design is spacious and thoughtfully laid out. My favorite exhibit, and one that's taken right from Florida's own backyard, is in the **Florida Wildlife Center**. If you're into manatees, the **Manatee Center** will absolutely knock your socks off. Look through the huge windows and see the gentle-giants swimming, playing, and munching on lettuce heads all day long. Manatees eat about one-hundred pounds of food a day. At the Lowry Park Zoo they eat lettuce and it costs them up to $30,000 per year, *per* manatee, to keep the zoo stocked in lettuce heads! (Consider that the next time you gripe about the cost of feeding your dog.)

Stroll through **Primate World** and see over fourteen of the species closest to man. Watch various monkeys, baboons, orangutans, and chimpanzees scattered throughout the natural setting. Note how "people-like" they are as they swing, roll, scratch, and play.

In the **Asian Domain** you'll encounter exotic animals including a sloth

bear, Sumatran tiger, Malayan tapir, and an Asian elephant. Check out the Indian rhinoceros–due to their near extinction, there are only thirty in the whole USA.

The free-flight **Aviary** is loaded with over sixty species of subtropical birds. Have a peek at white-bellied stork and the Malayan argus pheasant, but don't step on the tail of one the green iguanas slithering freely below.

Children love the **Children's Village**. In the petting zoo they can touch and communicate with gentle creatures like goats, sheep, pot-bellied pigs, rabbits, and a llama.

Age Range: Any age.
Hours: April through August from 9:30 a.m. to 6:00 p.m., daily; September through March from 9:30 a.m. to 5:00 p.m., daily. Closed Christmas.
Admission: Adults $6.50, seniors (50 and over), children (3-11) $4.50. Adult and child stroller rentals available.
Time Allowance: 2 to 4 hours.
Directions: From I-275 take the Sligh Boulevard exit and go west toward North Boulevard (4th traffic signal). Take a right onto North Boulevard and the zoo is ahead on the left.
Parking: Free.
Wheelchair Accessible: Yes.
Restaurant: Snackbar only, featuring native Florida cuisine.
Picnicking: No.
Rest Rooms: Yes.
Gift Shop: Yes, T-shirts, tote bags, and wild animal toys.
Cool Tip: Special zoo programs happen throughout the year for kids 2-7. How about a sleep-over with the manatees? What could be more fun?

MUSEUM OF SCIENCE AND INDUSTRY

4801 East Fowler Avenue
Tampa, FL 33617
(813) 987-6300

The dinosaur stuffed with garbage marks the entry to the Museum of Science and Industry (MOSI). The creative use of garbage reflects MOSI's approach to educating the public about the environment–in an imaginative, fun way. There are hands-on programs for all ages in topics ranging from astronomy to zoology.

Earthworks, on the second floor, is educational, eye-opening, and entertaining. Exhibits touch on conservation. Learn about water conservation through the toilet display (a favorite with kids). Q: How much water does it take to flush a toilet? Push the handle down on the resource-saving toilet and flush away. A: (only) one-and-a-half gallons of precious water. By the way, most toilets use *six* or *seven* gallons with each flush. What a waste! Think about how much water you use every day. Think about how all animals need that precious liquid to live.

A stroll through the free-flight **Butterfly Encounter** will remind you of how precious and fragile our planet is. Follow the life cycle of a butterfly and look at the butterfly chrysalises. It looks amazingly just like a leaf. See the colorful insects fluttering freely.

For something more disrupting, experience the

Gulf Coast Hurricane. Put on a pair of goggles, sit back, and get "blown away." The activity is scheduled hourly.

Kids under five enjoy **Kids in Charge**. It's a safe environment where kids are in control. Play with the giant blocks. Speak softly into the whisper tubes. Touch the fossils, snails, and shells. Or create a puppet show. You're the boss.

On the museum's third floor you'll find the **Planetarium** and **Communications Gallery**. The Planetarium offers hourly, forty-five-minute shows which familiarize you with outer space. The Communications Gallery is an interactive area where you learn about intercommunication through Morse code, whisper tubes, a truck with a CB radio, and computer monitors. Watch yourself on TV at the Channel 8 news studio!

Expect to see major expansions early in 1995 when MOSI triples in size. Among the additions will be **OMNIMAX**–a theater using the largest film frame in the history of cinema. Also featured will be **Bioworks**, a "living machine" used to treat the museum's *ten thousand gallons* of wastewater each day (a startling figure). By the way, most of the water at MOSI is cleverly recycled.

Age Range: Any age. "Kids in Charge" is designed for 5 and under.
Hours: Daily from 9:00 a.m. to 4:30 p.m.; Friday and Saturday until 9:00 p.m.
Admission: Adults $6.00, seniors (60 and up) and students with ID $5.00, children (2-12) $3.00.
Time Allowance: 3 to 4 hours.
Directions: From I-275 take Fowler Avenue (Exit 34) and proceed 3 miles east. From I-75 take Fowler Avenue (Exit 54) and go 2 miles west.
Parking: Free.
Wheelchair Accessible: Yes.
Restaurant: Snackbar only.
Picnicking: Yes.
Rest Rooms: Yes, with changing tables in women's room only.
Gift Shop: Yes; games, rubber snakes and spiders, tote bags.

CHILDREN'S MUSEUM OF TAMPA
7550 North Boulevard in Lowry Park
Tampa, FL 33604
(813) 935-8441

FUN SCALE

Don't let the size mislead you. There are a lot of educational, fun activities for younger kids, and it's a secure environment. What could be safer than **Safety Village**? The miniature 3-D replica of Tampa–or any city, really–is big enough for kids to scrunch down into and climb around. It's fully equipped with a bank building with fake money, an office building with real playable computers, a McDonald's restaurant with burgers and fries, a police station with handcuffs, and a library where kids can actually sign books out. Driving miniature cars and obeying stop signs, kids can learn about safety in the big city in a non-threatening way.

Step inside the museum and experience another culture. Classes in cooking, storytelling, and fitness are available throughout the year. The exhibits change annually and are based around various cultures. **Faces of the Americas** exposes you to the civilization of native American Indians through the sixteenth century. Step inside the adobe village and try a hand at weaving or grinding corn. Try on some of the ceremonial costumes. Learn about other ways to speak by listening to the language tapes. See that diversity and being different are okay. Everyone's special.

Age Range: Perfect for 3 to 8.
Hours: Monday through Thursday from 9:00 a.m. to 4:30 p.m., Friday from 9:00 a.m. to 3:00 p.m., Saturday from 10:00 a.m. to 5:00 p.m., Sunday 1:00 to 5:00 p.m.
Admission: $2.50 per person. Under 2 free.
Time Allowance: 1 or 2 hours.
Directions: From I-275 take Sligh Boulevard Exit and go east toward North Boulevard (4th traffic signal). Take a right onto North Boulevard.
Parking: Free.
Wheelchair Accessible: Yes.
Restaurant: No.
Picnicking: Yes, in park across street.
Rest Rooms: Yes, with changing tables.
Gift Shop: Yes, very small.

72

SALVADOR DALI MUSEUM
1000 Third Street South
St. Petersburg, FL 33701
(813) 823-3767

FUN SCALE

Melting clocks, androgynous people evolving from rocks, heads rising from piano keys, flowers escaping from egg shells... is it all a dream?

Explore the world of Salvadore Dali, the famous Spanish painter best known for his surrealistic images. This is the largest and most comprehensive collection in the world of his work. Paintings, drawings, photographs, and sculptures, are all exhibited in the museum.

Let your imagination run wild. Check out the interactive touchscreen computer.

Learn the background of surrealism. Take your time and wander around on your own, or hook up with a docent tour. Ask about one for the kids. These last for about an hour, run throughout the day, and reveal some of the hidden clues in Dali's work.

The museum has rotating exhibits about other artists who were relevant to Dali's work. Often student work based on surrealism is exhibited in the smaller gallery space. By the way, kids find surrealism a fascinating and inspiring style of art.

Age Range: 8 and up appreciate Dali's bizarre images, especially middle schoolers.
Hours: Tuesday through Saturday, 9:30 A.M. to 5:30 P.M. Sunday and Monday, 12:00 noon to 5:30 P.M. Closed Thanksgiving, Christmas, and New Year's Day.
Admission: Adults $5.00, seniors $4.00, students $3.50, children 9 and under free.
Time Allowance: 1 to 1 1/2 hours.
Directions: From I-275 to St. Petersburg take Exit 9 to Fourth Street South. Drive straight to Third Street South, turn right, and proceed to the Dali Museum on your left.
Parking: Free.
Wheelchair Accessible: Yes.
Restaurant: No, cafe next door.
Picnicking: Yes, across the street.
Rest Rooms: Yes.
Gift Shop: Yes, with all kinds of cool Dali mementos.

Copyright © Salvador Dali Museum

73

GREAT EXPLORATIONS
1120 Fourth Street South
St. Petersburg, FL 33701
(813) 821-8992

FUN SCALE

Turn the ordinary into the extraordinary. Stretch those mental muscles, fire-up the imagination, and experience **Great Explorations**. The hands-on museum has five permanent exhibits focusing on the arts, sciences, and health. In addition, rotating exhibits are brought in from museums around the world.

Start with **Phenomenal Arts,** where kinetic touch or audio activated activities deal in light through prisms and reflections. Create your own masterpiece on Light Strokes, a computer that creates a simulated image by painting with water. Create a symphony on the Ribbon Synthesizer. Touch the plasma balls and alter the patterns of light. Nothing is permanent but the printout from the Light Strokes computer.

Kids seven or older might consider a crawl through the **Touch Tunnel**. The ninety-six foot, pitch-black linear maze with various tactile surfaces gives you the experience of what it would be like to be blind. It could be an eye-opening experience–it was for me.

The **Think Tank** focuses on logic,

mathematics and physics, but don't let that scare you. The activities are designed for learning through fun. Discover the right combination to crack the safe. Find the way to untangle the ropes. Play left-right brain games.

Learn about the human body in the **Body Shop**. "How Old Are You Really?" "How Tall Are You?" "What's in Your Lunch?" These computer-activated testing stations increase body awareness.

Children six and under are fascinated by the **Explore Gallery**. It's full of safe, fun, child activities including an enterable giant fire truck with flashing red lights, costumes galore, a soft tunnel, a mini-puppet theater, and long tubes through which you can drop balls. Follow them through loops and curves until they reach the end.

The Exchange Pavilion contains multi-topic exhibits that change periodically. Call for current information.

Age Range: Any age. Explore Gallery is perfect for 6 and under.
Hours: Monday through Saturday from 10:00 A.M. to 5:00 P.M. Sunday from 12:00 noon to 5:00 P.M.
Admission: Adults $5.00, seniors (66 and older) $4.50, children (4-17) $4.00, children (3 and under) free.
Time Allowance: 2 to 3 hours.
Directions: From I-275 take Exit 9 to 4th Street South, turn right and the museum is a few blocks down on the left.
Parking: Free.
Wheelchair Accessible: Yes.
Restaurant: No.
Picnicking: Yes.
Rest Rooms: Yes, with changing tables.
Gift Shop: Yes; all kinds of cool T-shirts, science games, posters.
Cool Tip: On weekdays, visit from 12:00 noon to 5:00 P.M. to avoid school field trips.

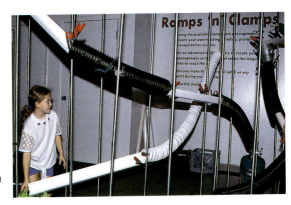

SUNCOAST SEABIRD SANCTUARY

18328 Gulf Boulevard
Indian Shores, FL 34635
(813) 391-6211

FUN SCALE

If you're planning to spend some time at this sanctuary, you'll need either a non-functioning sense of smell or to invest in a good pair of nose plugs.

Putting all odors aside, the bird shelter has a valuable mission–to rescue and rehabilitate seabirds. The viewable birds are all permanent residents, due to the nature of their injuries. The releaseable birds are not viewable, as they would become too domesticated and would not survive when re-released into the wild. The injuries result from oil spills, fishing line injuries, and being hit by cars, to name a few.

Great blue herons, owls, cormorants, pelicans, vultures, osprey, hawks–all are being cared for. You might want to have your cameras loaded.

Suncoast Seabird Sanctuary is a nonprofit rehabilitation center with a goal of educating the public and saving the birds. There's a true atmosphere of care and concern for the environment. By the way, the sight of the birds is worth dealing with the smell.

Age Range: Any age for varying amounts of time.
Hours: 9:00 A.M. to sunset.
Admission: Free, but donations accepted.

Time Allowance: About an hour.
Directions: From the St. Petersburg area, go west on Ulmerton Road until the end. Take a left on Gulf Boulevard and drive along the ocean for 4 miles until you see it on the right.
Parking: Free, but limited space.
Wheelchair Accessible: Yes.
Restaurant: No.
Picnicking: No, but two-hundred yards south along the beach is a public picnic area.
Rest Rooms: Yes.
Gift Shop: Yes; T-shirts, jewelry, bird books.

76

SUNKEN GARDENS
1825 Fourth Street North
St. Petersburg, FL 33704
(813) 896-3186

FUN SCALE

Within the walls of Sunken Gardens you'll find an abundance of birds and other animals surrounded by a carefully manicured botanical wonderland. Enter the garden and explore six acres of flora and fauna–from banana trees and poinsettia bushes to monkeys and wallabies. Stroll along the mile-long path that snakes through the splendor of tropical plants and experience a slice of Eden.

Hundreds of species from five continents fly freely in the **Aviary**; see birds up-close as you walk through it. Also scattered about the grounds are talking birds like "Joe," a scarlet macaw who has lived there for over fifty years. Don't touch the non-aviary birds–they bite. Try not to miss seeing one of the four scheduled **Bird Shows**. They run at 11:00 A.M., 12:30 P.M., 2:00 p.m., and 3:30 p.m. and offer lively entertainment.

There are pettable and feedable baby goats, but stay away from the baby gators. You might want to view the pot-bellied pigs from afar, too (peeuweee!).

While you're in the gardens, take a walk through the **King of Kings Wax Museum**. You'll see nine life-size scenes that depict the life of Jesus Christ from birth to resurrection. It's next to the gift shop and admission is free.

By the way, the name "Sunken Gardens" came about because the center of the gardens is twelve to fourteen feet below sea level.

Age Range: Although most of the guests are senior citizens, there's something for all ages, for varying amounts of time.
Hours: 9:00 A.M. to 5:30 P.M., daily.
Admission: Adults $11.00, children (3-11) $6.00. Stroller rentals for adults and children available.

Time Allowance: About 2 hours.
Directions: From I-275 take the 38th Street Exit heading east until you come to 4th Street North. Turn right, heading south on 4th Street North, and the garden is on the left.
Parking: Free.
Wheelchair Accessible: Yes.
Restaurant: Yes, and snackbar.
Picnicking: No.
Rest Rooms: Yes.
Gift Shop: Yes; jewelry, mugs, and knick knacks galore.

77

MOTE MARINE AQUARIUM
1600 Kenson Thompson Parkway
City Island
Sarasota, FL 34236
(813) 388-4441

FUN SCALE

It's as fascinating as it is educational to visit the Mote Marine Aquarium. Experience the sea creatures–from moray eels and spiny lobsters to tiger sharks and octopi (no, not in the same tank). Mote Marine Aquarium is dedicated to doing research, rescue, rehabilitation, and release. World renown marine research is conducted in exciting areas–cancer studies with sharks and skates, the effects of chemical pollutants on the environment, marine mammals and sea turtle studies, and water quality.

This is a kid-friendly environment. Youngsters are encouraged to touch the ocean creatures in the touch tank and ask the knowledgeable guides questions. Suddenly, the underwater world becomes accessible.

Take your time to explore the easily-viewable tanks. Mote has one of the country's premium shark facilities. Along with seeing the outdoor shark exhibit, touch the shark-skin display. Rub your fingers in one direction and then the other: Feel the difference! Look at the tiger shark's multiple rows of stark white teeth. You may ask why the teeth that you find on the beach are black–it's because they blacken as a reaction to the salt water; the reason why a living shark's teeth aren't black is because they loose and regrow their teeth on a regular basis.

Moving on to

the **Touch Tank**: Pick up a horseshoe crab and a starfish. Touch a sea urchin, but be careful–they're prickly. Try to touch a butterfly ray as it swims by. Lift a conch and a whelk shell. What's the difference? A conch shell opens on the right side and a whelk shell opens on the left!

The **Large Tank** contains sandbar sharks, sardines, and jewfish–to name a few. Look in through the window downstairs, walk upstairs, and peek down over the edge. Hold on to the kids!

Moving back inside, see sleek moray eels and spiny lobsters in the same tank; the lobsters look like sweet potatoes with legs. Learn about the symbiosis between the parchment worm and pea crab, or the clownfish and sea anemone. What unlikely couples! Check out the octopus, but don't tap on the glass. The disruption makes the octopus spray its ink and this poisons the water. Check out the miserable looking scorpion fish. It has a mug that only a mother could love!

Look, but don't touch the critters in the **Live Rock Tank**. See vividly colored corals and sponges, and don't forget the fact that they're *alive*. Explore the **Rivers, Bays, Estuaries** exhibit. From tidal fresh water turtles and eels to mangrove plants in the estuary, all are available for viewing.

At the end of your journey, you might choose to watch the fifteen-minute video (not much fun for kids) about the research that goes on at Mote. It's an ongoing video and is shown in the small auditorium near the gift shop.

Age Range: Any age.

Hours: 10:00 A.M. to 5:00 P.M., daily. Closed on Christmas, Easter, and Thanksgiving.

Admission: Adults $6.00, children (4-17) $4.00.

Time Allowance: 1 1/2 to 2 hours.

Directions: From I-75 take Exit 39 and go west on Rt. 780 (Fruitville Road). Cross U.S. 41 (Tamiami Trail) and continue west on the John Ringling Causeway (S.R. 789). At Saint Armands Circle take the first right and continue for 1 mile. It's on your right.

Parking: Free.

Wheelchair Accessible: Yes.

Restaurant: No.

Picnicking: Yes, with tables.

Rest Rooms: Yes.

Gift Shop: Yes; cool T-shirts, tote bags, rubber sea creatures.

RINGLING MUSEUM
5401 Bay Shore Road
Sarasota, FL 34243
(813) 359-5700

FUN SCALE

The name Ringling conjures up visions of the circus, and rightly so. However, along with being instrumental in bringing the circus to this country, John and Mable Ringling were major patrons of the arts and their winter estate is proof.

Sixty-seven acres are home to the **John and Mable Ringling Museum of Art**, the **Ca' d'Zan Mansion**, and the **Circus Gallery**.

Start with the **John and Mable Museum of Art**. The pink Italian Renaissance villa, decorated with columns, arches, fountains, and stained glass windows, creates a magnificent setting for an art museum. Venture inside and experience a rich collection of over five hundred years of European and American works. The collection includes one of the world's most impressive collections of Baroque paintings, and famous work by Rubens.

Enormous galleries contain intricately-detailed Flemish paintings from the seventeenth century, lovely nineteenth-century oriental fans, and an extensive twentieth-century collection of assorted media. Don't forget to stroll through the **Sculpture Garden Courtyard**. Standing

80

both powerfully and elegantly in the courtyard is one of the three copies in the world of Michaelangelo's sculpture *David*.

Fifty cents buys a *Self-Guided Activity Kit for Families*. The kit contains inspirational methods to spark kid's interests in art. Seven kits in total are available and range from a treasure hunt using a Rubens painting to a search for hidden messages in the Ca' D'Zan Mansion. (What better way to spend fifty cents?)

Ringling's winter house, **Ca' d'Zan Mansion**, (it means "house of John" in Venetian dialect), illustrates on a grand scale Ringling's love of Italy. It's visible as you walk through the terra cotta palace and find yourself surrounded by stained glass, marble terraces, painted ceilings, and ornately-carved furniture.

Getting back to the circus, don't miss the **Circus Gallery**. In 1948 the State of Florida chose to honor John Ringling by establishing a circus collection. Memorabilia include parade wagons, costumes, colorful posters, and a *Mini-Circus Show*. See the mini-reenactment of a circus with the lights, moving figures, an announcer, and circus music in the background.

Although guided tours are only available for groups on a pre-arranged basis, *Theme Tours* are given through the galleries Monday through Friday, though not during February and March. The *Annual Children's Festival*, with food, music, art projects, and gallery hunts is a big hit during February. Call for more information.

Age Range: 5 and up.
Hours: 10:00 A.M. to 5:30 P.M., Thursdays (October through June) to 10:00 P.M. The museum is closed on New Year's, Thanksgiving, and Christmas.
Admission: Adults $8.50, seniors (55 and over) $7.50. Children (12 and under) accompanied by an adult are admitted free.
Time Allowance: 2 to 3 hours.
Directions: From I-75 take Exit 40 and proceed west for 7 miles. Cross I-41 and you're there.
Parking: Free.
Wheelchair Accessible: Yes, but not the second floor of the Ca'd'Zan Mansion.
Restaurant: Yes. The Banyan Restaurant is open 11:00 A.M. to 4:00 P.M. October through June; and 11:00 A.M. to 3:00 P.M. July through September.
Picnicking: Yes; I would suggest sitting in front of the Ca'd'Zan Mansion along the water.
Rest Rooms: Yes.
Gift Shop: Yes; jewelry, stationary, and objets d'art.

SARASOTA JUNGLE GARDENS
3701 Bayshore Road
Sarasota, FL 34243
(813) 355-5305

FUN SCALE

These lush gardens were started over fifty years ago on a swampy banana grove. Tropical flora was collected from around the world and, over the years, exotic animals were added to create a place where you could experience and learn about a wild environment. Safari through the formal gardens and jungle trails of the ten-acre complex. See monkeys, flamingos, a huge tortoise, wallabies, and two beautiful silky-black and sadly-caged leopards.

The twenty-five minute **Reptile Show** first presents a video about reptiles and the dangers of poisonous snakes. An alligator section follows, with eye-opening information that destroys fallacies about these most primitive of living reptiles.

The twenty-minute **Bird Show** exhibits endless talents, from macaws riding bicycles and doing somersaults to cockatoos roller-skating and taking IQ tests. See the fifty-seven year-old cockatoo named "Frosty" ride a unicycle. Awesome! Both shows run throughout the day.

Children two to six will find endless pleasure in the **Kiddie Jungle**. It's truly a wonderful playspace where kids can slide down the back of a giant dragon, climb a tree with a trunk-face and branch-arms and swing from its branches, and pretend to be the conductor of a giant choo-choo train. Also check out the small **Petting Zoo** in the same area, and pass through the **Shell and Butterfly** exhibits.

Age Range: Any age. Kids 2-6 will enjoy Kiddie Jungle.
Hours: 9:00 A.M. to 5 P.M., daily.
Admission: Adults (13 and up) $8.00, children (3-12) $4.00.
Time Allowance: About 2 hours.
Directions: From I-75 take the University Parkway Exit and head west until you come to the end.

Turn left on I-41 and proceed for about 2 miles. It's on your left.
Parking: Free.
Wheelchair Accessible: Yes.
Restaurant: Snackbar only.
Picnicking: Yes.
Rest Rooms: Yes.
Gift Shop: Yes; rubber alligators, pens, posters.

BABCOCK WILDERNESS ADVENTURE
8000 State Road 31
Punta Gorda, FL 33982
(813) 489-3911

FUN SCALE

Imagine an area that's six times the size of Manhattan, but without Manhattan's high-rise buildings, pollution, and crime. Fill it with 90,000 acres of oak hammock, pine woods, pastures, swamps, and wetlands. Add wild animals flying, swimming, and roaming about. You've just entered the Babcock Wilderness Adventure.

Hop on a giant swamp buggy and watch the woods come alive. Take the ninety-minute narrated tour and discover dozens of wild alligators, Florida panthers, American bison, cows, white tailed deer, and wild turkeys scattered throughout the wooded areas. Both the panthers and bison are in protected areas, but the fencing isn't visible. At one point during the tour a touchable baby alligator is brought on board (for those who feel the need to see up-close and touch a gator).

Don't forget to make your reservations in advance.

Age Range: 5 and up.
Hours: January through April tours run every half hour from 9:00 A.M. to 3:00 P.M., daily. May through October tours offered morning hours only, and the site is closed on Mondays and alternate Sundays. November and December tours run at 9:00 A.M., 11:00 A.M., 1:00 P.M., and 3:00 P.M., daily. Call for precise times as they vary depending on demand. Reservations necessary.
Admission: Adults $15.95, children (3-12) $7.95.
Time Allowance: Tour lasts about 1 1/2 hours.
Directions: Traveling *south* on I-75, take Exit 29 and head east on S.R. 74. Turn right at Babcock Corner on S.R. 31, and head south for six miles. It's on your left. (From Exit 29 on I-75 it's about 23 miles.) Traveling *north* on I-75 take Exit 26 and head east on S.R. 78. Turn left on S.R. 31 and head north for six miles. It's on your right. (From Exit 26 on I-75 it's about 11 miles.)
Parking: Free.
Wheelchair Accessible: No.
Restaurant: No.
Picnicking: Yes.
Rest Rooms: Yes.
Gift Shop: Gift cart with T-shirts, jars of honey, and post cards.

EDISON/FORD WINTER ESTATES

2350 McGregor Boulevard
Fort Myers, FL 33901
(813) 334-7419

FUN SCALE

Anyone who pooh-poohs the Edison/Ford Winter Estates as being a stuffy place for old folks to visit should think twice. Yes, Thomas Edison is a no longer alive, but his inventions live on. Take the half-mile walking tour and visit Edison's home, laboratory, and museum.

Thomas Edison (1847-1931) was a prolific inventor in his day. Most famous for the invention of the incandescent lamp and phonograph, Edison developed over one thousand patents dealing with electronics, batteries, cement, and motion pictures. His light bulbs still burn today and his phonographs, although in a different form, still bring music to our ears.

Enter Edison's elegant **winter home** and step into an era gone by. The estate house is decorated with early American furniture. Traces of his many inventions fill the rooms. The electric chandeliers were made in his workshop. The very same lightbulbs made by Edison are still used today; they burn twelve hours every day and have never burned out!

In the **museum**, discover four rooms containing the finest collection of Edison's inventions. Among the extensive collection see antique phonographs, movie projectors, a ticker tape machine, and lightbulb upon lightbulb. Listen to the first "talking doll"–a favorite among the kids. Look at the collection of old vehicles and see a Model T Ford given to Edison by Henry Ford, an old Cadillac, and a three-horse fire pumper.

Step into the **chemical laboratory** where Edison conducted many experiments. The lab remains today just as he left it, with test tubes in racks,

labeled bottles, beakers of mysterious liquids, and his cot for late-night "cat naps." He was also an extraordinary botanist and his plant dabblings brought him to the discovery of a new source of rubber–a goldenrod filament.

Stroll through the extensive **gardens** and discover walls of brilliant bougainvillea, herald's trumpet covering an entire top of a fifty-foot mango tree, banyan trees that seem to spread forever, coffee plants, African sausage trees, and passion flowers, to name a few. April is the most colorful month to see blossoms in.

A longtime friend of Thomas Edison, **Henry Ford** (1863-1947), purchased the house next door in 1916. Take the quarter-mile walking tour through **Ford's winter home** and grounds. See the spot where the Fords hosted wild square dances, the windows through which they watched captivating birds, and the automobiles for which Ford is known. The display contains a 1914 Model T with a hand crank, a 1917 Model TT truck with an oak cab, and a touring car complete with a trunk. The trunk is literally strapped to the back of the car!

Age Range: 8 and up.
Hours: Monday through Saturday 9:00 A.M. to 4:00 P.M., Sunday 12:30 P.M. to 4:00 P.M. Last tour leaves at 3:30 P.M. Closed Thanksgiving and Christmas.
Admission: Adults $10.00, children (6-12) $5.00.
Free stroller use available. Limited quantities.
Time Allowance: About 2 hours.
Directions: From I-75 take Exit 22 and follow Rt. 884 (Colonial Boulevard) west until it ends on MacGregor Boulevard. Turn right and it's ahead on the right.
Parking: Free.
Wheelchair Accessible: Yes.
Restaurant: No.
Picnicking: Yes.
Rest Rooms: Yes.
Gift Shop: Yes; post cards, books, light bulb gizmos.

IMAGINARIUM
The Hands-on Museum and Aquarium
P.O. Box 2217
Fort Myers, FL 33902
(813) 332-6666

FUN SCALE

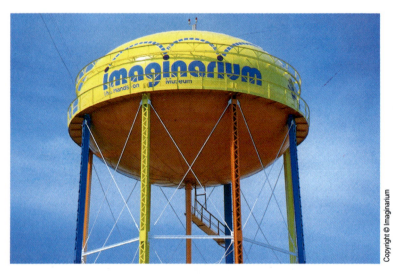

Copyright © Imaginarium

Located at the historic and converted water treatment plant in Fort Myers, the extraordinary interactive Imaginarium Hands-on Museum and Aquarium has eleven acres of exciting exhibits designed to stir the imagination and motivate the sense of wonder.

Phase One of Imaginarium takes place in **Edison Hall**, which contains exhibits designed to stimulate curiosity, with learning as the outcome. Kids are encouraged to explore topics ranging from health to business. Climb through pieces of hair that are taller than you in *Healthy Bodies*. Sink some basketballs in the *Physical Endurance Room*. Learn about the effects of drunk driving in *Car Crash*. Experience a simulation of what it would be like to drive under the influence of one drink, two drinks... a valuable and frightening experience.

Rock-out with a selection of musical instruments from the *Music Wall*. Climb aboard the *Emergency Medical Vehicle* and play the role of a paramedic. Step into the *Production Studio* and broadcast the news. Temporarily freeze your shadow on the wall in *Shadow Freeze*. Make deposits and withdrawals at the automatic teller machine in the *Bank*. You're never too young to earn and spend money!

A **Touch Tank** sits in the main lobby and, among other squiggly creatures, contains shrimp and anchovies. Also in the main lobby is the **Everglades and Gulf of Mexico Aquarium** composed of living animals native to the area.

Copyright © Imaginarium

Some grand plans are in the works for future interactive sights. Phase Two, scheduled to open in the fall of 1995, is geared for older kids. It will consist of an **Everglades Habitat**–a walk-through exhibit, and **Land, Sea & Air**–hands-on meteorology, oceanography, and TV studio work. Phase Three, scheduled to open in the fall of 1996, will be called **Hall of Inventions** and will house exhibits geared for everyone.

Age Range: Phase One is geared for all ages, Phase Two is projected for older kids (middle and high school), and Phase Three is targeted for all.

Hours: Tuesday through Saturday 10:00 A.M. to 5:00 P.M., Sunday 1:00 to 6:00 P.M. Closed Monday.

Admission: Adults $6.00, children (3-12) $3.00.

Time Allowance: 2 to 4 hours.

Directions: From I-75 take Exit 23 and proceed west on Dr. Martin Luther King Jr. Boulevard. It's on the corner of King Boulevard and Cranford Street. Look for the huge water tower as a landmark.

Parking: Free.

Wheelchair Accessible: Yes.

Restaurant: Yes.

Picnicking: Yes, with tables.

Rest Rooms: Yes, with changing tables.

Gift Shop: Yes; science kits, T-shirts, games.

CARIBBEAN GARDENS
(Jungle Larry's)
1590 Goodlette Road
Naples, FL 33940
(813) 262-5409

 FUN SCALE 🎈🎈🎈🎈

First of all, to clear things up a bit, Caribbean Gardens *is* Jungle Larry's–but with a new name. While most still refer to it as Jungle Larry's, which it was, it is *really* currently named Caribbean Gardens.

The fifty-two-acre site of lush tropical greenery is laced with pathways. You might begin your safari with a **Tram Tour**, a twenty-five minute introduction, which is good, but not as much fun for kids as hoofing around on their own two feet.

Another option is to go on the **Safari Island Cruise**, which takes you on a boat out to the primate habitats. Primates live uncaged on the islands and frequently entertain the cruise people by swinging from vines, climbing trees, and picking bugs from each other's backs. Check out the ring tailed lemurs from Madagascar as they circle the island. It's a relaxing twenty-minute boat ride and well worth your time.

An array of wild animals from Africa, Asia, and South America are scattered about the tropical forest. Stroll through the banyan trees, stately palms, and rustling bamboo, and find animals including lions, leopards, anteaters, alligators, monkeys, and cockatoos.

Various animal shows, including an **Elephant Demonstration,** a **Leopard Act,** an **Alligator Feeding**, and an

Animal Antics Show happen at scheduled times throughout the day. Don't miss the **Big Cat Show**. See the six monstrously beautiful *cats*, as they stand on their awesome hind legs awaiting raw-meat rewards.

Scheduled to have opened in the fall of 1994 are the **Clouded Leopard Forest** and **Reflection Point.** You will be able to enter the forest and surround yourself with leopards with dark spots (cloud-shaped) on a gray and yellow background; you'll feel as if you're in the wilds of Nepal or Borneo. In the pavilion at **Reflection Point,** you will be able to view the rare and endangered jungle species from above. Also planned is a restaurant to be housed inside the pavilion.

The **Petting Zoo** is a fun stop for younger children. Take a ride on an elephant for $2.50.

Age Range: Any age.
Hours: 9:30 A.M. to 5:30 P.M., daily. Ticket office hours are 9:30 A.M. to 4:00 P.M. Closed Thanksgiving and Christmas.
Admission: Adults $10.95, children (4-15) $6.95.
Time Allowance: 3 to 4 hours.
Directions: From I-75 take Exit 16 heading west on S.R. 896 (Pine Ridge Road). Take a left on S.R. 851 (Goodlette Road), and continue south for about 4 miles until you see it on your left.
Parking: Free.
Wheelchair Accessible: Yes. Free wheelchairs are available. Strollers rent for $2.00 per day.
Restaurant: Snackbar only.
Picnicking: Yes, with tables.
Rest Rooms: Yes, with changing tables.
Gift Shop: Yes; games, T-shirts, rubber reptiles, and post cards.

TEDDY BEAR MUSEUM
2511 Pine Ridge Road
Naples, FL 33942
(813) 598-2711

FUN SCALE

The teddy bears around the world owe a moment of silence to the man after whom they were named–President Theodore Roosevelt. As the story goes, Teddy Roosevelt, while out on a hunting expedition, chose to spare the life of a baby cub. The press caught wind of it and immortalized the event with a cartoon. From then on it was history–and so was the term "teddy bear."

Bears, bears, they're everywhere! From whimsical to serious, from antique "do-not-touch" to modern "snuggleable," all live within the museum walls. Have you ever seen a tree house full of mini-teddies? Or a teddy bear picnic–complete with ants? Or a school scene where mischievous grizzly students are anything but attentive and have placed a thumbtack on the teacher's chair?

Climb inside the "Three Bear's Cottage" and pretend to be Goldilocks. Push the button on Bingo Bear and hear him say silly things like, "Will you scratch my back?" Sit down at the board of directors table with giant stuffed pandas and imagine a very important meeting in process. Look up and see teddies floating in a giant hot air balloon or even riding a Ferris wheel. Everywhere you look, a teddy looks back at you. Most of the teddies are behind glass and "untouchable," but certain designated bears are, as they say in museumland, "playable."

Various classes and workshops are given throughout the year, on such topics as storytelling, jewelry making, bear making, and bear repairing.

Age Range: 3 through 10 is ideal.
Hours: Wednesday through Saturday 10:00 A.M. to 5:00 P.M., Sunday 1:00 to 5:00 P.M.
Admission: Adults $5.00, seniors and teens $3.00, children (4-12) $2.00.
Time Allowance: About 1 hour.
Directions: From I-75 take Exit 16 and go west for 1 1/2 miles on Pine Ridge Road. The museum is on the right before the intersection with Airport Road.
Parking: Free.
Wheelchair Accessible: Yes, with 2 loaners available.
Restaurant: No.
Picnicking: Yes, but beware of fire ants.
Rest Rooms: Yes, with changing tables.
Gift Shop: Yes; teddy bears!

KEY WEST AQUARIUM
1 Whitehead Street
Key West, FL 33040
(305) 296-2051

FUN SCALE

It's not the biggest and most flashy of aquaria, but it *is* one of the three oldest in the country. On display in large tanks are fishes found in the local waters of the Atlantic, Caribbean, and Gulf of Mexico. Included in the collection are a wide variety of sharks, exotic tropical fish, green turtles, and lobsters.

Embark upon a **guided tour** and expand your knowledge of the ocean. During the thirty-minute tour, you'll listen to experts expose mysteries of the deep. You'll witness sharks being hand-fed and, possibly, *touch* a shark. Speaking of touching, check out the **Gulf Shore Touch Tank**. Grab a slimy sea cucumber or a prickly sea urchin. Examine a hermit crab or a horse conch. Pick up a triton's trumpet and touch a starfish.

Age Range: Any age.
Hours: 10:00 A.M. to 6:00 P.M., daily. Guided tours given at 11:00 A.M., 1:00 P.M., 3:00 P.M., and 4:30 P.M.
Admission: Adults $6.00; children (8-15) $3.00; children 7 and under free, but must be accompanied a paying guest; seniors, military, and students with I.D. receive $1.00 off adult admission.
Time Allowance: 30 to 90 minutes.
Directions: Follow U.S. 1 south almost all the way to the end. U.S. 1 turns into Truman Avenue. Seven blocks down Truman Avenue, you'll see on your right the Lighthouse Museum. Turn right on Whitehead Street just after the Lighthouse Museum. The aquarium is eight blocks ahead on the right.
Parking: Free.
Wheelchair Accessible: Yes.
Restaurant: No.
Picnicking: Yes.
Rest Rooms: No, but nearby.
Gift Shop: No.

THEATER OF THE SEA
P.O. Box 407
Islamorada, FL 33036
(305) 664-2431

FUN SCALE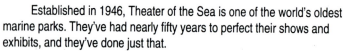

Established in 1946, Theater of the Sea is one of the world's oldest marine parks. They've had nearly fifty years to perfect their shows and exhibits, and they've done just that.

Expose yourself to the fascinating world of marine animals. Experience a close-up encounter with big fish and squiggly creatures. The general admission includes the **Sea Lion Show** and **Dolphin Show**. Take a guided **Walking Tour** and see sharks, dolphins, and sea turtles up close. Learn how to handle sea life properly. Pick up a sea cucumber or sea anemone. (Slimy!) Climb aboard the bottomless boat and see dolphins at play surrounded by a spectacular coral reef lagoon.

The **Dolphin Adventure** can be *viewed* by children twelve and under, but only people thirteen and older can partake in the actual *swimming* with the dolphins. An orientation seminar is followed by the swim session with the dolphins. It's a wonderful chance to spend thirty minutes in the water, surrounded by–and even touching–dolphins.

Copyright © Theater of the Sea

Age Range: Any age will enjoy the dolphin and sea lion shows, and touch tanks; the Dolphin Adventure Package is for 13 and older.
Hours: 9:30 A.M. to 5:45 P.M., daily; ticket office closes at 4:00 P.M.
Admission: General Admission for adults $12.25, children $6.75.
Dolphin Adventure Package–$75.00 per person (13 and older); advance reservations required. *Show and observation only*–Adult $14.00, children (3-12) $8.50.
Time Allowance: 1 to 2 hours
Directions: Take U.S. 1 to mile marker 84 1/2.
Parking: Free.
Wheelchair Accessible: Yes.
Restaurant: Snackbar only.
Picnicking: Yes, on the patio outside of the park.
Rest rooms: Yes, with a changing table in the women's room.
Gift Shop: Yes.

VENETIAN POOL
2701 De Sota Boulevard
Coral Gables, FL 33134
(305) 460-5356

FUN SCALE

Nestled behind pastel stucco walls and wrought iron gates is a special and secretive oasis-like find. In 1923 a coral rock quarry was transformed into a beautiful swimming pool. Decorated with a vine-covered portico, a palm-fringed island, a cobblestone bridge, a waterfall, and a sandy beach, it's more than just a swimming hole. It's a slice of history with a Mediterranean feel.

The water, because the pool is fed by underground artesian wells, is a constant and pleasant seventy-six to seventy-eight degrees throughout the year. Various water programs including aerobics, scuba diving, and swimming lessons are available throughout the year. Lifeguards are always on duty.

Age Range: Any age. There's a shallow sectioned-off area for the non-swimmers.
Hours: *Weekdays*–Mid-June through mid August 11:00 A.M. to 7:30 P.M.; September/October and April/May 11:00 A.M. to 5:30 P.M. (closed Monday); November through March 11:00 A.M. to 4:30 P.M. (closed Monday). *Saturday and Sunday* (year round) 10:00 A.M. to 4:30 P.M.
Admission: *Non-residents*–Adults $4.00, teens (13-17) $3.50, children (12 and under) $1.60. Babies 12 months and under are not permitted in the pool. *Coral Gable Residents*–Adults $3.00, teens (13-17) $2.00, children (12 and under) $1.60.
Time Allowance: 1 hour to full day.
Directions: Although confusing, the Venetian Pool *is* findable. Find Coral Way (a major east/west road in Coral Gables). Take a left on De Soto Boulevard (between Toledo and Segovia). It's a couple of blocks down on the left.
Parking: Across the street and free.
Wheelchair Accessible: Yes.
Restaurant: Cafe only.
Picnicking: No.
Rest Rooms: Yes; with showers inside and out.
Gift Shop: No.

93

AMERICAN POLICE HALL OF FAME
AND MUSEUM
3801 Biscayne Boulevard
Miami, FL 33137
(305) 573-0070

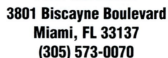

FUN SCALE

You can't miss the building–it's the one with the police car dangling from its side. Step inside and open your eyes to the American Police Hall of Fame's fascinating and moving displays. "Dedicated to the men and women nationwide who 'serve and protect,' " the institution houses captivating memorabilia and sends out clear messages.

Begin with a solemn walk through the **Police Memorial**, a room dedicated to police killed on duty. Inscribed with names and towns, the marble walls are also decorated with cards, photos, and flowers in vases; it is similar in feeling to the Viet Nam Memorial in Washington D.C. The list of names numbers some five thousand and counting.

See the vehicle display–from typical cruisers to the brilliant orange sportscar used in *Bladerunner*, the movie. Climb onto the back of a real police motorcycle.

Go upstairs and look at the displays of weapons, ranging from common street pistols to plastic play guns. See the gruesome display of Tommy guns beside photos of people killed by these machines of destruction. See the same style Italian rifle that Lee Harvey Oswald used to kill John F. Kennedy in 1963. Do you know he had ordered it through a mail order catalogue? (Kind of makes you think, doesn't it?) Another disturbing display of weapons asks this

question: "If a young man, child, or even an adult faced you with any of these weapons displayed, would you fire your own gun first?" A startling thought.

Pretend to be Sherlock Holmes in the **Crime Scene Room**. Investigate the scene of the crime, carefully scour the room full of evidence, and solve the case. Those who do will get an official certificate declaring them to be super sleuths.

For more hands-on displays, step inside the prison cell or gas chamber. Sit in the electric chair and have a friend strap you in. Check out the guillotine and stocks.

Age Range: 4 and up.
Hours: 10:00 A.M. to 5:30 P.M., daily. Closed Christmas.
Admission: Adults $6.00, seniors $4.00, children (under 12) $3.00.
Time Allowance: 1 or 2 hours.
Directions: From I-95 take the exit for I-195 going east. Take the second exit (Biscayne Boulevard). It's on the corner of 38th Street and Biscayne Boulevard.
Parking: Free, and there's a guard in the lot.
Wheelchair Accessible: Yes.
Restaurant: No.
Picnicking: No.
Rest Rooms: Yes.
Gift Shop: Yes; postcards, caps, clothing.

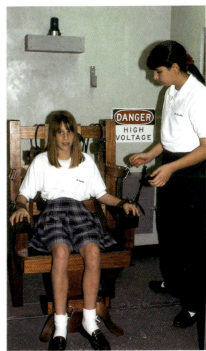

CORAL CASTLE

28655 South Dixie Highway
Homestead, FL 33034
(305) 248-6344

FUN SCALE

The story is phenomenal. Edward Leedskalnin, after being heart-broken by his girlfriend, set out to build a monument dedicated to his unrequited love. In doing so, the Latvian immigrant, who was born in 1887, created the most bizarre structure this side of the Mississippi. Keep in mind that Edward was five feet tall and weighed only one hundred pounds. Rejected in romance, he spent twenty years carving massive pieces of coral and turning them into master works of art. During that time, he carved and moved over 1,100 tons of coral without human assistance. (*¡Que romantico!*)

Venture inside and push the nine-ton gate open; it's so perfectly balanced that it can be opened with one finger. Climb the coral (of course) steps to Leedskalnin's rustic living quarters. Explore the results of a project that occupied twenty years of his life: A table, hand-carved, in the shape of Florida, and reading chairs that were positioned by the sun's changing hours. His interest in the universe sparked creations of sun dials, moons, and a sculpture of Saturn. Push the buttons at each of four sites to activate the audiotapes. They're in English, French, German, and Spanish, and are loaded with interesting facts.

Coral Castle reminded me of Stonehenge, the massive monument in England, which was constructed around 2000 B.C. as a ritual site and ancient calendar. Both display magnificent feats of human strength and diligence driven by an obsession or belief. Curiously enough, Edward Leedskalnin wasn't even aware that Stonehenge existed.

In 1936 the sculptures were transported by tractor from Florida City, where Leedskalnin lived and did the carving. The move took three years. Isn't it amazing that, alone, one broken-hearted man carved structures of such monumental proportions? The Coral castle has mystified scientists as well as psychologists since it was opened to the public.

Age Range: 8 and up.
Hours: 9:00 A.M. to 7:00 P.M., daily. Closed Christmas.
Admission: Adults $7.75, seniors $6.50, children (7-12) $5.00.
Time Allowance: About an hour.
Directions: From Miami, take Rt. 1 south and turn left on S.W. 286th Street. It's on your left.
Parking: Free.
Wheelchair Accessible: Yes, but not upstairs in the living quarters.
Restaurant: No.
Picnicking: Yes.
Rest Room: Yes.
Gift Shop: Yes; coral jewelry, grapefruit trees, postcards.

EVERGLADES ALLIGATOR FARM
40351 Southwest 192nd Avenue,
Homestead, FL 33034
(305) 247-2628

FUN SCALE

Copyright © Everglades Alligator Farm

Out in the Hurricane Andrew devastated area of Homestead, lies Dade County's oldest alligator farm. And it *is* an actual alligator farm.

Look at the **breeding ponds** where the females build nests, mate, and lay eggs. Each female lays up to fifty eggs. (Yikes, imagine if they each lived!) The eggs are then placed in an incubator and hatched. Interestingly enough, the temperature of incubation determines the sex of the baby gator. Temperatures of about eighty degrees produce a female and about ninety degrees produce a male–fascinating!

The **grow-out pens** house the gators, from one month to four years old. Baby gators can grow as much as three feet during their first year. Their brains will reach only the size of a lima bean. Alligators are fed raw chicken, fish, or nutria. A nutria is a large, promiscuous rodent found in Louisiana, where the multiplying population is a problem. The Louisianans are more than happy to send them off to the Florida gator farms. Alligators also absolutely *love* marshmallows!

Climb aboard the speedy **airboat**, stuff the complimentary cottonballs in your ears (its jet engines can be pretty loud), and you're off, into the mysterious Everglades hammock. The thrilling thirty-minute glide over and through shallow water and reeds takes you past Florida's native creatures–osprey, snowy egrets, soft-shell turtles with pointy snouts, catfish,

98

bass, and, of course, alligators.

Various shows happen throughout the day. Cross the bridge to **Snake Island** and see the *Snake Show*. View the viper and cower at the cobra. See the seventy-five-pound python named "Monty" wrapped around his trainer's neck. *Gator Shows* and *Gator Feedings* also occur at scheduled times throughout the day. Generally, after the shows, a gator or snake is available for touching. Cameras ready!

Age Range: Any age.
Hours: 9:00 A.M. to 4:30 P.M., daily.
Admission: *Farm and Airboat Ride*–Adults $11.00, seniors $10.00, children (4-12) $3.00. *Farm Only*–Adults $5.00, seniors $4.00, children (4-12) $3.00.
Time Allowance: About 2 hours.
Directions: From Miami go south on U.S. 1 until S.W. 344th Street (Palm Drive) and take a right. Drive 2 miles and take a left on S.W.192nd Avenue. Continue for 4 miles. It's on the left.
Parking: Free.
Wheelchair Accessible: Yes, but on farm only. (Airboats are not wheelchair accessible.)
Restaurant: Snackbar only.
Picnicking: Yes.
Rest Rooms: Yes.
Gift Shop: Yes; T-shirts, rubber gators, and insect repellent.

METROZOO
12400 Coral Reef Drive
(Southwest 152nd Street)
Miami, FL 33177
(305) 251-0400

FUN SCALE

Although still showing devastation from Hurricane Andrew, the Metrozoo is, slowly but surely, making repairs and renovations. It's *still* a gigantic (290-acre) site for exciting exploration and learning.

Take a safari into the wild. From ant eaters to zebras, all creatures can be observed in their own cageless environment. There's only a moat separating you from most of the animals. Choose from a multitude of viewing options: monorail, tram, your own two feet, wheelchair, stroller, piggy-back...

The air conditioned **Zoofari Monorail Ride** takes you on a half-hour tour, stopping at four stations, and is included in the price. It's a good way to get an overview. The **Personalized Tram Tour** takes you on a narrated, in-depth visit with the animals. Or, you may opt to cover the three to four miles of trails via foot, which is actually a better way to get up-close to the creatures.

Young children will want to head straight for **PAWS**, the petting zoo. Kids can feed and interact with baby deer, sheep, lizards, pot bellied pigs, rabbits, and even ride an elephant. Check out the scorpion and tarantula cages–*not* pettable parts of the petting zoo!

The zoo is organized by geographic areas of the planet. See a homely *marabou stork* that rests uncomfortably with its legs bent backwards. Catch a view of a *bay duiker*, a skittish antelope the size of a rabbit. Gaze at the sloth-like *water monitor,* a lizardous-looking animal that's as big as a five-year-old alligator, but much scarier looking. See the strikingly-sleek *Bengal tigers*–two of only 150 remaining in the world. Check out the stately *giraffes* that seem to float as they run across the fields. Ogle over the cuddly *Bennett wallabies.* Admire the awesome *African elephants.* Make your way around the park and experience the foreign creatures who, surprisingly enough, are from the same planet–Earth.

Catch a scheduled show at either the **Children's Zoo** or the **Amphitheater**. They run regularly throughout the day and include *Wildlife Shows* and *Elephant Performances.*

Age Range: All ages.
Hours: 9:30 A.M. to 5:30 P.M., daily. Ticket booth closes at 4:00 P.M.
Admission: Adults $5.00, children (3-12) $2.50.
Time Allowance: 3 to 4 hours.
Directions: Take I-95 south to U.S. 1 south. Turn right on 152nd Street and proceed until you come to 124th Avenue. Turn left and it's ahead on the left.
Parking: Free.
Wheelchair Accessible: Yes.
Restaurant: Snackbars only.
Picnicking: No.
Rest Rooms: Yes.
Gift Shop: Yes; T-shirts, stationary, stuffed animals.

MIAMI SEAQUARIUM
4400 Rickenbacker Causeway
Miami, FL 33149
(305) 361-5705

FUN SCALE

Remember Flipper? The superstar TV hero is still alive and flipping at Miami Seaquarium, as are many other sea celebrities.

Six different shows, presented continuously throughout the day, include the **"Flipper" Show**. Flipper, a remarkably intelligent dolphin, is joined by other marine friends to entertain with a campy beach party, a castaway scene, and an aquatic football game. Throughout the show, trainers give lively explanations of both the behavior and biology of dolphins.

For a truly awesome experience, step into the **Killer Whale Show**. Lolita, the mammoth black and white killer whale weighs about 8,000 pounds and eats about 200 pounds of raw fish a day. She splashes (and I mean *splashes*) around the tank demonstrating her remarkable athletic abilities. She flukes, flips, spins, and then chomps on fish rewards. When she performs, she sends whale-sized walls of water at unsuspecting visitors in the first few rows. So be forewarned!

At the **Golden Dome Sea Lion Show** some silly antics are performed under a spherical structure designed by the architect Buckminster Fuller. Here, sea lions and seals conduct a sea rescue, balance a soccer ball on their noses, perform in a comical skit, and shout louder than imaginable asking for food rewards.

Check out the **Top Deck Dolphin Show** and see dolphins jump, flip in the air, swim on their sides, showing their pectoral fins, and spin through the water. Bebe, the thirty-seven year-old dolphin, sleekly shows off her athletic abilities through incredible aerial acrobatics. Listen to them communicate with the trainers through dolphin talk.

Learn more about sharks through the **Shark Presentation**. Watch big fish hanging from the bridge get chomped by the much-feared creatures. Listen to the trainer destroy some of the rumors about sharks. Not to imply that they're *not* dangerous, many more people die as a result of venomous snake bites than shark encounters.

Sea Life Touch Pools offer a chance to touch starfish and other slimy creatures. Feel stingrays glide by gracefully as you carefully touch a sea urchin.

The big shows listed above were operational when I visited, but Hurricane Andrew had caused severe damage and a number of the exhibits were closed. Slowly but surely, the displays are being renovated and put back to use.

Age Range: Any age.
Hours: 9:30 A.M. to 6:00 P.M., daily. Ticket booth closes at 4:30 P.M.
Admission: Adults $17.95, children (12 and under) $12.95.
Time Allowance: 3 to 5 hours to see all of the shows.
Directions: From I-95 take the exit for Key Biscayne. Follow the Rickenbacker Causeway to the Seaquarium, which is on the right.
Parking: Free.
Wheelchair Accessible: Yes.
Restaurant: Snackbars only.
Picnicking: No.
Rest Rooms: Yes, with changing tables in women's rooms only.
Gift Shop: Yes; T-shirts, film, stuffed animals.

MIAMI YOUTH MUSEUM

Bakery Centre, 5701 Sunset Drive
Third Floor
South Miami, FL 33143
(305) 661-ARTS

FUN SCALE

Situated in Miami's Bakery Center, a shopping center that hasn't yet become popular, the Miami Youth Museum (M.Y.M.) has, nevertheless, made it into the realm of popularity. It provides a space for kids to play, create, imagine, touch, see, and learn through discovery.

The M.Y.M. is divided into three areas: a theater for live performances, and two exhibit spaces divided by age range. **Kidscape**, the exhibit space for younger kids (three to eight), contains an interactive mini-community which encourages children to experiment with certain real-life situations. The *Winn-Dixie Supermarket* is built with a child's size in mind–everything is reachable! Learn about counting and choosing healthy groceries. *Dr. Smile's Dental Office* allows the child to play in a dentist's office, which possibly will alleviate some of the anxiety common in that area, and, at the same time, learn how to take care of those pearly whites! The *Metro-Dade Fire Station* encourages kids to learn about fire safety by dressing in real fire-fighter gear, climbing aboard the fire truck, and playing with authentic equipment on the fire rescue vehicle.

The exhibit space for older kids (nine to twelve) utilizes more sophisticated equipment for interaction. *Metro-Dade Police Safe Neighborhood* is designed to acquaint people with what's involved in police work. Climb into the squad car. Learn about the importance of sober driving. Make your own

fingerprints on an official fingerprint pad. The *Channel 4 News Exhibit* is a working studio where kids can explore the world of broadcast news. They become news reporters right in front of the cameras and learn TV is an important tool for communication.

The exhibits change regularly, but there is always something of interest and value for the youngsters. Kids must be accompanied by an adult.

Age Range: 3 to 10, possibly 12.
Hours: Monday, Friday, Saturday, and Sunday 10:00 A.M. to 5:00 P.M. Tuesdays and Thursdays 1:00 P.M. to 5:00 P.M. Open during all school holidays (Monday through Friday) 10:00 A.M. to 5:00 P.M.
Admission: $3.00 per person.
Time Allowance: 1 to 2 hours.
Directions: From Miami, south on U.S. 1 and exit left on 57th Avenue (Red Road). Take the first right and park on the third floor of the lot. Walk across the bridge and you're there.
Parking: Pay-lot. $1.00 per hour. $3.00 maximum.
Wheelchair Accessible: Yes.
Restaurant: No, but close by.
Picnicking: No.
Rest Rooms: Yes.
Gift Shop: Yes; T-shirts, posters, pencils.

MONKEY JUNGLE

14805 Southwest 216th Street
Miami, FL 33170
(305) 235-1611

FUN SCALE

"Where humans are caged and monkeys run wild!" reads the sign. And it's right! What a twist–you're in the screened walkway surrounded by primates. Nearly four hundred primates inhabit the thirty-acre reserve.

Enter, and you're immediately surrounded by monkeys crawling curiously on the fence and going about their daily routines. About one hundred *Java Macaques* roam freely throughout the jungle. They're skilled skin divers in the wild. Watch them dive into the pool and collect crabs. See tiny *Golden Lion Tamarins*, native to Brazil and threatened with extinction, play in the natural surroundings. See *Colubus monkeys* playing with their babies. Reach out and feed the primates peanuts and raisins through wires. The fact that you're allowed to get so close to them adds to the intrigue of the Monkey Jungle.

A variety of primate shows happen throughout the day. **Chimpin' with Colin and Colleen** offers about twenty minutes of chimpanzee antics. The only thing predictable about the silly twin chimps is that they're always unpredictable. In **Hangin' with Orangs** you'll meet Lucy and Mei, two easily trainable apes. Watch them perform for food rewards. Some monkeys love the water. See them wade and skin dive during the **Wild Monkey Swimming Pool**

Show. A favorite is the **King of Our Jungle Show**. It is truly amazing to meet "King," the enormous lowland gorilla, and see how closely he resembles humans.

Age Range: 3 and up.
Hours: 9:30 A.M. to 5:00 P.M., daily.
Admission: Adults $10.50, children (4-12) $5.35.
Time Allowance: About 2 hours.
Directions: From the Florida Turnpike take Exit 11 to S.W. 216th Street and go west for 3 1/2 miles.
Parking: Free.
Wheelchair Accessible: Yes.
Restaurant: Snackbar only.
Picnicking: Yes.
Rest Rooms: Yes.
Gift Shop: Yes; T-shirts, books, puzzles.

MIAMI MUSEUM OF SCIENCE AND PLANETARIUM

**3280 South Miami Avenue
Miami, FL 33129
(305) 854-4247**

FUN SCALE

Hop on a bicycle and pedal like mad to activate the generator that drives the train around the tracks. The faster you pedal, the faster it goes. Turn into an archaeologist and uncover hidden fossils in the sandpit. Push a button to activate an engine and watch its parts move. These are just a few of the

possibilities for exploration at the Miami Museum of Science and Planetarium.

Step into **The Body in Action** and learn about the kidney on a computer or muscle flexibility on the muscle-measuring machine. Push a button and watch the bones move as a human skeleton pedals a bicycle.

Walk through the **Wildlife Center** and explore a living collection of more than 175 animals. See the humongous Galapagos tortoise, a stately bald eagle, and an ominous-looking vulture. Stroll through the aviary, and see an enclosed space brimming with owls and other birds that have been wounded and can't fly.

Spectacular changing shows highlight the museum. When I was there, *"The Miami Herald ROBO BUGS!™ Giant moving Insects"* fantastically filled the gallery space with big, frightening creatures. The bugs moved their heads, crunched their mandibles together, and rose high above the heads of the visitors as we gazed up in awe. On a more serious note, *What About Aids?* was an informative exhibit that educates both adults and kids about the deadly disease. Other rotating shows, ranging from *Greenhouse Earth* to *Finding Your Way and the Amazing Monster Maze* occur throughout the year.

The **Miami Space Transit Planetarium** offers regularly scheduled shows highlighting activity in the universe. Shows run throughout the day. For the older kids, **Laser Shows in the Planetarium** is shown on weekend nights.

108

Rock-out laserly to music from Pink Floyd to Led Zeppelin.

On the first Saturday of each month, weather permitting, the planetarium hosts a free star lecture followed by star gazing.

Age Range: 4 and up.

Hours: 10:00 A.M. to 6:00 P.M., daily; box office closes at 5:00 P.M. Closed Thanksgiving and Christmas.

Admission: *Museum Only*–adults $6.00, seniors (62 and up) and children (3-12) $4.00.

Planetarium–adults $5.00, seniors and children $2.50.

Laser Show–adults $6.00, seniors and children $3.00.

Combination–adults $9.00, seniors and children $5.50.

Time Allowance: About 2 hours.

Directions: From I-95 *south* take Exit 1 (Key Biscayne Boulevard) and follow the brown signs. Traveling *north* on I-95, turn right at the giant sloth which is just before U.S. 1.

Parking: Free.

Wheelchair Accessible: Yes.

Restaurant: No.

Picnicking: Yes.

Rest Rooms: Yes, with changing tables.

Gift Shop: Yes; T-shirts, games, books.

PARROT JUNGLE AND GARDENS
11000 Southwest Miami Avenue
Miami, FL 33156
(305) 666-7834

FUN SCALE

Parrot Jungles and Gardens combines a spectacular collection of tropical plants, trees, and flowers with exotic birds and animals. Clean and attractively designed grounds set the stage for shows held throughout the day and exhibitions.

Nestled in the tropical rain forest, the wildlife theater is the site of **Wildlife Shows** featuring Florida's native animals. The *Trained Bird Shows* occur in the all-weather amphitheater and should not be missed. See parrots like "Paco" raise the American flag and "Macho" pedal a chariot across the

110

stage. "Marty the Macaw" takes a psychology test by matching colored shapes–and he aces it!

Stroll leisurely through the gardens and see an array of tropical plants–from cacti to sausage trees. You can't miss the humongous banyan tree; its aerial roots seem to spread for miles.

Flamingo Lake is the place to see zillions of brightly colored flamingos. They're fed daily at 3:00 p.m. and, speaking of food, their diet consists of shrimp. Shrimp contain a certain carotenoid that produces that brilliant pink in their feathers; otherwise, flamingos would be a beige-pale-pink color.

Set your children free in the **Playground and Petting Zoo**. It's a place where they can lean over the fence and feed and pet goats, pigs, deer, and birds. It's also a place to burn excess energy on the jungle gym equipment.

Don't miss the **Primate Playground**. You'll see an assortment of baby orangutans and chimps rolling around and playing with each other. The fact that they're wearing diapers adds to their cuteness.

Age Range: Any age.
Hours: 9:30 A.M. to 6:00 P.M., daily.
Admission: Adults (13 and older) $10.95, children (3-12) $7.95. Strollers available at $2.00 rental fee.
Time Allowance: 2 to 3 hours.
Directions: Take U.S. 1 south to SW 112th Street (Killian Drive). Continue west for 2 miles. It's on the left.
Parking: Free.
Wheelchair Accessible: Yes, with wheelchairs available for free.
Restaurant: Snackbar only.
Picnicking: No.
Rest Rooms: Yes.
Gift Shop: Yes; T-shirts, pot holders, games.

VIZCAYA MUSEUM AND GARDENS
3251 South Miami Avenue
Miami, FL 33129
(305) 579-2708

FUN SCALE

Copyright © Vizcaya Museum and Gardens

A trip to Vizcaya Museum and Gardens means a journey back to the splendor of the sixteenth century. Resting magnificently at the edge of Biscayne Bay is this twenty-eight acre tract of land containing an Italian Renaissance-style villa surrounded by over ten acres of formal gardens, a native mangrove, and a hardwood hammock. Built between 1914 and 1916 by the American industrialist James Deering (co-founder of International Harvester Company), it functioned as a tropical winter home. He delighted in collecting art from many major eras of European history–Neoclassic, Rococo, Baroque, and the Renaissance. Paintings, sculpture, tapestries, and ornate furniture decorate the villa.

Hook up with an informational forty-five-minute guided tour; feel free to jump in at any point or start from the beginning. The guide leads you (ground

Copyright © Vizcaya Museum and Gardens

floor only), explaining the history of the villa, and is more than willing to answer questions. This is a good way to hear some interesting trivia, and to learn about otherwise unknown pieces of art.

Walk around and imagine what it would have been like living in an estate like Villa Vizcaya. The sea horse was declared one of the symbols of Vizcaya and is found engraved and painted on various pieces of art throughout the house. See if you can spot them. Look at the oddly-shaped, adjustable fire screens. As the story goes, a lady's makeup back then was made of wax and

would melt if she sat near the fire. The conveniently-adjustable screen protected the woman's makeup from melting. (Yikes!) Step into **Renaissance Hall** and see the very same seats that former President Ronald Reagan and the Pope John Paul II sat in during a visit to Vizcaya. Climb the spiral staircase and check out the ornate bird cage on the second floor. There's no bird now, but even the birds led the life of luxury! Don't forget to look up at the intricate ceilings; they too are spectacular.

After touring the house, step outside and explore the formal grounds. You'll see an Italian fountain surrounded by waterways leading to smaller fountains. Walk through the **Maze Garden** and the **Reflecting Pool Garden**. Don't miss sauntering through the **Secret Garden**.

By the way, the name "Vizcaya" is a Basque word meaning "an elevated place."

Age Range: 8 and up. Nothing is hands-on.
Hours: 9:30 A.M. to 5:00 P.M. Ticket booth only closes at 4:30 P.M., gardens at 5:30 P.M. Closed Christmas Day.
Admission: Adults $8.00, children (6-12) $4.00.
Time Allowance: About 1 1/2 hours.
Directions: From I-95 south take Exit 1 and follow signs for Vizcaya.
Parking: Free.
Wheelchair Accessible: Yes, ground floor and gardens only.
Restaurant: Cafe only.
Picnicking: Yes.
Rest Rooms: Yes.
Gift Shop: Yes; slides, calendars, Italian tapestries.

BUTTERFLY WORLD

3600 West Sample Road
Coconut Creek, FL 33073
(305) 977-4400

FUN SCALE

Copyright © Butterfly World

Kids love butterflies. They're magical. Enter the world of nature's most colorful insect in the free-flight environment at Butterfly World. Get there early, because butterflies are "solar powered" and are much more active from the morning until about 3:00 p.m. See butterflies and moths flutter about the lovely landscaped three-acre garden.

The most magical of the three aviaries is the **Tropical Rain Forest** exhibit. Walk in and fill your eyes with colorful butterflies, ring neck turtle doves, banana and palm trees, and gigantic and colorful carp swimming in a pond below. Listen to the water falling over the rocks and the sounds of life buzzing in the air. Every five minutes a light tropical rain shower refreshes the butterflies and unsuspecting visitors. Look out!

Learn about butterflies in the **Pupa Emerging Area**, where you can witness the miracle of life as the butterflies emerge right before your eyes. See the entire lifecycle through lab windows in the *Butterfly Farm*, and check out the collection of insects, butterflies, and moths from every corner of the globe in the **Museum/Insectarium**.

When butterflies are active, they flutter from plant to plant, to nectar blossoms for pollen, and to caterpillar food plants on which to lay their eggs. The eggs hatch and turn into caterpillars, which turn into butterflies, which lay more eggs... and the cycle continues. Think about the lifespan of the butterfly: They live from three days to three months, but the average lifespan is only about a week.

Age Range: Any age, with different amounts of time. Most children love butterflies.
Hours: Monday through Saturday 9:00 A.M. to 5:00 P.M., Sunday 1:00 to 5:00 P.M. Admission gate closes at 4:00 P.M.
Admission: Adults $8.95, seniors $7.95, and children (3-12) $5.00.
Time Allowance: 1 to 2 hours.
Directions: Take I-95 or the Florida Turnpike to Sample Road and follow the signs for Butterfly World.
Parking: Free.
Wheelchair Accessible: Yes.
Restaurant: Snackbar only.
Picnicking: Yes.
Rest Rooms: Yes.
Gift Shop: Yes; jewelry, butterfly nets, mugs.

FLAMINGO GARDENS
3750 Flamingo Road, Davie/Fort Lauderdale, FL 33330
(305) 473-2955

FUN SCALE

Take the half-hour narrated **Tram Tour**, and cruise through luscious smelling citrus groves, the native hammock, and rich wetland areas. See Florida as it was a century and a half ago. You will hear interesting facts about the state's rich history, and be stimulated by the garden's lovely smells and sights.

The **Citrus Collection**, which includes both commercial and ornamental varieties, is extraordinary. Tangelos (a combination of grapefruit and tangerine), oranges, lemons, limes, grapefruits, kumquats, and even banana trees grow in the Eden-like environment. At the right time of year, the buds smell absolutely heavenly.

Set off on foot, or in a stroller or wheelchair, and discover the other sixty acres of the gardens. Stroll through the grounds and visit the **Hibiscus Garden**, a colorful grow space with hibiscus plants–from miniatures to double giants. The **Iris Garden** contains vibrant species that are easily grown in the area. The **Xeriscape Garden** demonstrates plants that grow well in a low maintenance, minimal irrigation area; low water and succulent plants such as cacti and aloe vera grow here. The **Hummingbird Garden** contains flowering plants such as impatience and oleander, with nectar that drives hummingbirds wild.

116

A walk through the acre **Aviary** is a must. The screened enclosure contains five separate ecosystems including the coastal prairie, mangrove swamp, cypress forest, sawgrass marshlands, and subtropical hardwood hammock. See ninety species of colorful birds, including blue herons and storks, fluttering and flapping about. Many have been taken under the wing of Flamingo Gardens because they've been injured. For a little respite from the heat, step into the air conditioned **Aviary Classroom**. There's a huge picture window for easy aviary viewing.

Speaking of flamingos, don't forget to see the **Flamingo Island Habitat**. The blazing red birds live on an island amid tropical vegetation and sparkling waterfalls. They maintain their color from a diet of shrimp and other forms of red carotenoids. (Not a bad life–meals of shrimp on an island in the tropics!)

If watching curious and small water animals conducting their daily chores is your fascination, don't miss the **River Otter Habitat**. Next to the Iris Garden lies the **Crocodilian Lagoon** where both alligators and crocodiles, from three to twelve feet, swim in harmony. Yes, gators and crocs *can* live together, but they *never* crossbreed.

Age Range: Any age.
Hours: 9:00 A.M. to 5:00 P.M., daily.
Admission: Adults $8.00, seniors and students with ID 20 percent off, children (3-11) $4.50.
Time Allowance: 2 to 3 hours.
Directions: From I-95 take the exit for I-595 or S.R.84 and proceed west to Flamingo Road. Turn south for 3 miles on Flamingo Road.
Parking: Free.
Wheelchair Accessible: Mostly.
Restaurant: Snackbar only.
Picnicking: Yes.
Rest Rooms: Yes.
Gift Shop: Yes; T-shirts, gift fruit shipping, orange tree kits.

OCEAN WORLD

1701 Southeast Seventeenth Street
Fort Lauderdale, FL 33316
(305) 525-6612

FUN SCALE

Hundreds of swimming, sliding, flopping, and splashing creatures greet you the moment you enter Ocean World. You're surrounded by an array of exhibits and performances by both people and sealife. Get close to the action.

Shows run non-stop throughout the day and include sessions with sea lions, dolphins, and exotic birds. The six scheduled shows run one at a time, allowing you to go from show to show, and not miss a thing.

In **Sea Lion Training,** the playful Pinnipeds demonstrate their frisky and inquisitive nature combined with their capacity for memory and agility. Sea lions communicate vocally and, at times, can be very vociferous. The show's climax happens when the massive sea lion balances on one flipper, supporting six hundred pounds of weight. Awesome!

The **Exotic Bird/River Reef** performance displays an assortment of tropical birds from toucans to parrots. Hear a macaw bark like a dog, quack like a duck, and say "hello" to the audience–much like a person.

Both dolphin shows are worth your while. The **High Flying Dolphins** exhibit takes place in the state-of-the-art Dolphin Habitat that provides a natural environment for the park's thirteen Atlantic bottlenose dolphins. Gaze into the eyes of a dolphin. Save the spectacular and action-packed **High Flying Dolphins** show for last. Watch the dolphins swim and do tricks with

their trainers. The triple flip is absolutely spectacular. Those viewers in the front should get set to get wet. The dolphins are frisky and splashy when motivated by fishy rewards.

At an extra cost you can spend an hour aboard *Miss Ocean World*, and cruise the canals of Fort Lauderdale, where you can see mansions of the wealthy and their gleaming yachts. The cruise is narrated with plenty of jokes. A snackbar and gift shop are available on board.

Age Range: Any age.
Hours: 10:00 A.M. to 6:00 P.M., daily.
Admission: Adults $11.95, children (4-12) $9.95. *Miss Ocean World*–adults $6.00, children (4-12) $5.00.
Time Allowance: 2 or 3 hours.
Directions: From I-95 take the exit for Davie Road (Rt. 82), and proceed east until you reach U.S. 1. Head south on U.S. 1 and turn left on 17th Street. Ocean World is ahead on the left.
Parking: Free.
Wheelchair Accessible: Yes, all but the third floor of the High Flying Dolphin Show. That show can be viewed from the portholes below.
Restaurant: Snackbars only.
Picnicking: No.
Rest Rooms: Yes.
Gift Shop: Yes; T-shirts, jewelry, rubber sharks.

MUSEUM OF DISCOVERY AND SCIENCE

401 Southwest Second Street
Fort Lauderdale, FL 33312
(305) 467-6637

FUN SCALE

Copyright © Museum of Discovery and Science

Learn about the fascinating world in which you live. The modern Museum of Discovery and Science allows you to refresh your mind and exercise your brain–all under the same roof.

Florida Ecoscapes spans most of the first floor and delves into the ecology of Florida. The exhibit includes a *Beach* where visitors can play with rays and other creatures in the touch tank. The *Grotto* contains moray eels. In *Sloughs and Swamps*, you'll find native toads, frogs, and alligators. Listen to the sounds in the walk-in *Beehive*, which is encased in a simulated cypress tree.

Should you choose to explore the **Choose Health** exhibit, you'll learn about three areas: fitness, nutrition, and substance abuse. *Activity Challenges* is designed to acquaint people with the relationship between activity and wellness. *Thought For Food* provides stimulation through a simulated supermarket. *Substance Alert* exposes shocking views of a real diseased lung and presents a video on the effects of drugs.

"What's *that*?" you ask. Located on the second floor, the **Sound** exhibit educates viewers through ears-on attractions including *Animal Voices, Chladni Plates,* and *Kaleido Vision*–a walk-in kaleidoscope.

120

No Place Like Home presents a "cutaway" home designed to increase consumer awareness about the environmental effects household products and wasting our natural resources will have on the Earth's future. See inside an oven, toilet, and air conditioner. Learn how they operate. Don't forget to challenge yourself with the interactive quiz asking questions pertaining to specific areas of the house.

Astronauts at heart will love **Space Base**, designed to teach people about space flight and the exploration of space. Included in the display are simulated rides. The *Manned Maneuvering Unit* challenges the visitor to perform simple tasks under a gravity-free environment. (Weight and height restrictions apply.) The *Moon Voyager* simulates a trip to outer space in a small vessel. Learn about how astronauts function in outer space.

Kidscience is a must for children ages three through five. They can set their natural curiosities free on various hands-on activities ranging from walking on a musical staircase to enveloping yourself in a giant walk-in bubble maker.

For 2-D action that gives the appearance of being 3-D, **Blockbuster IMAX Theater** creates experiences, including a trip to *Anarctica* and a live *Rolling Stones* concert, on a sixty-by-eighty-foot screen in a five-story room,

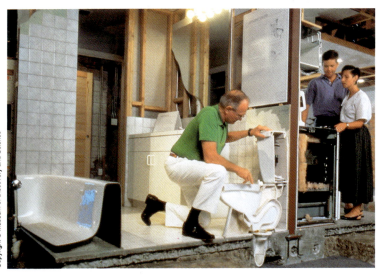

with sound from forty-two speakers. You're surrounded with the audio and visual excitement of glaciers, guitars, valleys, and clouds. It's almost a sensation-overload!

This museum is huge, it's fun, and more than worthwhile. In fact, I touched a live boa constrictor that was wrapped around the neck of one of the guides. I saw live bats under red lights flying from fruit kabobs to branches and back again. I saw an enormous grouper, appropriately named "Boomer," swimming around in the tank. I heard a startlingly-real sounding mosquito buzzing through binaural headphones.

It's a playground for both the mind and senses.

Copyright © Museum of Discovery and Science

Age Range: Any age. Kid Science is perfect for kids 3-5.
Hours: Monday through Friday 10:00 A.M. to 5:00 P.M.; Saturday 10:00 A.M. to 8:30 P.M.; Sunday Noon to 5:00 P.M. Closed Christmas.
Admission: *Museum*–adults $6.00, seniors (65 and over) and children (3-12) $5.00.
IMAX Theater–adults $5.00, seniors and children $4.00.
Combination–adults $8.00, seniors and children $7.00.
Time Allowance: About 2 hours for the museum alone. Times for IMAX shows vary.
Directions: From I-95 take the Broward Boulevard Exit and drive east to S.W. 5th Avenue (Commodore Brook Street). Turn right and the museum is on your left.
Parking: Huge metered lot across the street.
Wheelchair Accessible: Yes.
Restaurant: Snackbar only.
Picnicking: Yes, in the food area.
Rest Rooms: Yes, with changing tables.
Gift Shop: Yes; T-shirts, volcano kits, maps.

CHILDREN'S SCIENCE EXPLORIUM
Royal Palm Plaza, Suite 15
131 Mizner Boulevard
Boca Raton, FL 33432
(407) 395-8401

FUN SCALE

Here is a wonderful place where you can be both challenged and surprised by the world of science.

Discover the attractive qualities of a magnet and learn about how a **compass** works. Generate **electricity** by pedaling a bicycle. Pull on the rope, raise the dowel, blow, and create a gigantic bubble on the **Bubble Machine**—an ingenious contraption. Put your hand on the plasma globe and see a mini-lightening flash. Walk into the **Frozen Shadow Room**. *Click*, your silhouette is frozen on the wall, but then it disappears. Put your hands on the **Van de Graaf** generator and watch your hair go wild. Talk about a "bad hair day" nightmare-come-true! Design beautiful works of art in the **Computer Room**. Make a print of your masterpiece at no extra charge. Roll the ball down the **Gravity Track** and watch it loop before dropping on the floor. Step in front of **Jacob's Ladder** and watch the sparks fly.

The only thing the Children's Science Explorium is lacking is space. There's a lot to explore, but not much area for examination.

Age Range: 3 to 12.
Hours: *Summer*–Sunday through Friday Noon to 5:00 P.M.; Saturday 10:00 A.M. to 5:00 P.M. *Winter*–Tuesday through Saturday 10:00 A.M. to 5:00 P.M., Sunday 12:00 noon to 5:00 P.M. Closed Monday.
Admission: All ages $2.00.
Time Allowance: 1 or 2 hours.
Directions: From I-95 take the Palmetto Park Boulevard Exit and proceed east until you come to Mizner Boulevard (past the Federal Highway). Turn right and it's on the right in the Royal Palms Plaza.
Parking: Free.
Wheelchair Accessible: Yes.
Restaurant: No, but nearby.
Picnicking: No.
Rest Rooms: Yes.
Gift Shop: Yes; stickers, science kits, post cards.

123

GUMBO LIMBO
ENVIRONMENTAL COMPLEX
1801 North Ocean Boulevard
Boca Raton, FL 33432
(407) 338-1473

 FUN SCALE

First opened in 1984 as a nature preserve, the Gumbo Limbo Environmental Complex sits on one of the few surviving coastal hammocks in South Florida.

Step inside the Complex's original building and learn about the natural history of the area. Put your hand in the **Feel Box.** What's inside? A manatee rib? A coconut shell? Don't worry, they took the live snakes out years ago!

Match the names with the photos on the **Birds of Southern Florida Board**. Push the button and see if you're right. Feel the **eastern diamondback rattlesnake skin**. Rub your hand in one direction and it's rough, and in the other and it's smooth. See the **live snakes** in tanks. Explore the **working bee hive**.

Step outside and explore the four open aquaria: **Shallow, Deep**, **Tide**, and **Swirl Tanks**. They hold sea turtles, sharks, and other regional sealife.

Walk through the **Boardwalk Trail** and see why it's noted as being similar to a coastal hammock during the days of Ponce de Leon in the early sixteenth century. Read the names of the trees as you go. The gumbo limbo, alias "tourist tree," is always red and peeling. Can you figure out why they call it the "tourist tree?" Climb the tower and gaze out at the spectacular view.

You're above the treetops, and can see the Atlantic Ocean on one side and the Intracoastal Waterway on the other.

Sea turtle research is an important part of the Complex. In April the turtles lay their eggs, and the turtle specialists go out and cover them with protective cages. The eggs then hatch in sixty days. The baby turtles are challenged to find the water, and often get disoriented. This is where the turtle savers come to their aid and head them in the right direction.

All sorts of nature programs are offered throughout the year, from early morning beach combing to collecting marine life. **Beach turtle walks** are a favorite. In fact, the sign-up day takes place on the first Saturday in May and, within two hours, the whole summer is booked!

Age Range: Any age.
Hours: Monday through Saturday 9:00 A.M. to 4:00 P.M.; Sunday 12:00 noon to 4:00 P.M.
Admission: Free.
Time Allowance: 1 or 2 hours.
Directions: From I-95 take the exit for Palmetto Park and go east until it ends. Turn left on Ocean Boulevard (A1A) and go north for 1 mile. It's on your left.
Parking: Free.
Wheelchair Accessible: Yes.
Restaurant: No.
Picnicking: No, but across the street it's allowed.
Rest Rooms: Yes.
Gift Shop: No.

CHILDREN'S MUSEUM
498 Crawford Boulevard
Boca Raton, FL 33432
(407) 368-6875

FUN SCALE

Housed in Singing Pines, the oldest house in Boca Raton (it was built in 1914), the Children's Museum allows children to enjoy the house's history and explore some modern-day challenges in an intimate playspace.

The **Pioneer Kitchen** (the only non hands-on section of the museum) allows you to experience a sliver of the past. What would it have been like back then to prepare a meal in those conditions?

Sample a taste of banking at the museum **Mini-bank**. Poke around in the child-size vault and pay with the pink and blue "kidscash." You might take your money around the corner to the **Xtra's mini-supermarket**. Learn about shopping for food. Push the cart up and down the aisles and select your nutritionally-balanced, wholesome meal. Be careful not to take too much and stay away from that candy! Ring it up at the cash register. Bag it. And take it home. (Well, not really, put it back on the shelves for the next shopper.)

Also, check out the changing exhibits–from trains and musical instruments to dinosaurs.

Age Range: Great for 3 to 6. Older kids would be bored. There are "Traveling Museum" outreach programs for kids up through sixth grade, but the in-house museum exhibits are more appropriate for the younger children.

Hours: 12:00 noon to 4:00 P.M., Tuesday through Saturday. Closed major holidays.

Admission: Adults $1.00 (suggested donation), children $1.00.

Time Allowance: About an hour.

Directions: From I-95 take Palmetto Parkway Exit and head east to Crawford Street. Turn left on Crawford Street. It's ahead on the right.

Parking: Free.

Wheelchair Accessible: Yes.

Restaurant: No.

Picnicking: Yes.

Rest Rooms: Yes.

Gift Shop: Yes, small.

DREHER PARK ZOO
1301 Summit Boulevard
West Palm Beach, FL 33405
(407) 533-0887

FUN SCALE

The Dreher Park Zoo operates on twenty-two acres of tropical gardens and holds over one hundred different species of animals. Snake along the paths through and past exhibits of **South Florida**, **Asia**, **South America**, and **Australia**. Each displays animals native to their area, including several endangered species.

Bengal tigers, creatures of rare beauty, are among those on the endangered list. See the startlingly beautiful white tiger with black stripes and blue eyes. No vegetarians, Bengal tigers in the wild kill prey and eat up to sixty-five pounds of meat in one feeding. Their roar can be heard up to two miles away. Awesome!

Younger children (8 and under) will appreciate **A.R.K. (Animals Reaching Kids)**. This is where the touchable animals live. Drop 25¢ into the vending machine, let the grain spill into your hand, and feed the furry animals. Reach out and pet a miniature *horse*, *llama*, *zebu*, *donkey*, *bunny rabbit*, or *sheep*.

The short but sweet **Nature Trail Boardwalk** winds around a peaceful lake. See what Florida looked like fifty years ago. Animal life consists mostly of fowl and deer. For an extra $1.00 per person, you can take a cruise around the lake on a pontoon boat–a pleasant experience.

Age Range: Any age.
Hours: 9:00 A.M. to 5:00 P.M., daily. Call for summer and holiday hours.
Admission: Adults $5.00, seniors (60 and up) $4.50, children (3-12) $3.50.
Time Allowance: About 2 hours.
Directions: From I-95 take Southern Boulevard or Parker Boulevard east to Parker Avenue. Take Parker Avenue to Summit Boulevard and proceed west for 1/2 mile.
Parking: Free.
Wheelchair Accessible: Yes.
Restaurant: Snackbar only.
Picnicking: Yes.
Rest Rooms: Yes, changing table in women's room.
Gift Shop: Yes; T-shirts, stuffed animals, games.

LION COUNTRY SAFARI

P.O. Box 16066
West Palm Beach, FL 33416
(407) 793-1084

FUN SCALE 🎈🎈🎈🎈🎈

Where else would you see signs like "Elephant Crossing" or "Yield to Leaping Gazelles"? Lion Country Safari offers a 500-acre "cageless" wildlife preserve with over one thousand wild animals from all over the world. Lions and tigers roam freely, and people are in their cars. What a twist!

The **Gorgonza Preserve** is where the lions roam. Don't be fooled by the fact that they look like cuddly kittens–keep the windows up! In **Wanki National Park** you'll come eye-to-eye with giraffes, zebras, and rhinoceroses. These animals aren't car-wise; they saunter and leap across the road. Be careful of the llamas: They're slow and tend to hog the road, and they don't recognize car horns either.

Watch the primates play on their island habitat. The fact that monkeys have no body fat and would sink in the water, makes them content to stay on the island. According to Dr. Jane Goodall, the chimpanzee expert, the **Chimp Islands** and the other primate displays are "the finest natural displays of wild chimpanzees in the world outside of Africa."

The **Serengeti Plains** is habitat of the African elephant and other hoof stock. Check out the nilgai or "blue bull," largest of Asian antelopes. This funny creature looks like a huge blue cow with blue-gray skin. Don't be too surprised if a African

128

ostrich decides to stick its nose in your window. They're curious–and nosy creatures!

After visiting the preserve, continue on into the **Safari World Amusement Park**. All activities are free, and all are fun for kids yearning for some hands-on action. The **Great American Farmyard Petting Zoo** allows you to feed llamas, goats, lambs, and other gentle animals. If you're into reptiles, check out the gators, crocs, snakes, and lizards; if not–or even if you are–ride an old-fashioned carousel, play miniature golf, or take a paddleboat tour around the lake.

Age Range: Children 8 and older might appreciate the drive-through preserve more than the park, and younger kids might appreciate the hands-on part of the park more than the preserve, but there's no definite division.

Hours: 9:30 A.M. to 4:30 P.M., 365 days a year.

Admission: Adults $11.95, children (3-15) $9.95.

Funky looking zebra-striped *rental cars* with air conditioning are available (for those with convertibles or other unacceptable safari vehicles) at $5.00 per hour. Pets aren't allowed in cars during safari. *Kennels* are provided at no extra charge.

Time Allowance: 3 hours to full day.

Directions: From I-95 take exit for Southern Boulevard and go west for fifteen miles. It's on the right-hand side.

Parking: Not applicable–you tour in your car. However, at the amusement park there is a free lot.

Wheelchair Accessible: Yes.

Restaurant: Snackbar only.

Picnicking: Yes.

Rest Rooms: Yes, with changing tables.

Gift Shop: Yes; T-shirts, tote bags, stuffed animals.

Cool Tip: Catch the lions at the right time (generally morning or late afternoon), and you'll see them playing friskily together and gnawing on a piece of meat.

129

SOUTH FLORIDA SCIENCE MUSEUM

4801 Dreher Trail North
West Palm Beach, FL 33405
(407) 832-1988

FUN SCALE

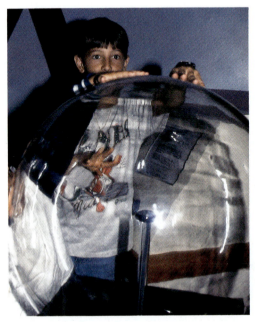

"Suzie," a twenty-two thousand year-old juvenile *mastodon,* greets you as you enter the South Florida Science Museum. Turn the corner and you're confronted by a massive *sperm whale jaw bone.* Watch the mysteries of light, energy, and the environment come alive through the use of the museum's interactive exhibits and displays.

Step into the **Light and Sight Hall**, and learn about color perception and optical illusions. Enter the *Frozen Shadow Room.*

Pose. Wait. Your silhouette is on the wall, and then it's gone. Look at the mysterious *Holograms.* The basket of eggs is so real, you can almost reach out and touch it. Dracula rises right out of his casket in an alarming and convincing action. Put your hands on the *Plasma Globe* and move the light rays. Create electricity with your own bare hands. Check out *Jacob's Ladder* and see what 110 volts of house current looks like.

A special place and favorite of mine is the **Living Reef Exhibit**. Sit down in the dark room and surround yourself with vibrantly-colorful ocean creatures. The immaculately-clean and well-lighted tanks provide the perfect atmosphere for viewing *nurse sharks*, *moray eels*, and *skunk shrimp*–to name a few. By the

130

way, the skunk shrimp chomp on the algae and other dirty deposits in the tanks, helping to keep them clean.

Just outside of the aquarium is a **Touch Tank**. It's small, but contains an array of colorful sea specimens. Reach in and gently pick up a *sea urchin;* they're not as scary as they look. Let a *ray* brush by your hand. Slimy!

In the **Aldrin Planetarium**, you'll travel through the solar system, galaxy, and universe without leaving your seat. A hands-on component is included in the meteor show, bringing the lesson down to Earth. The *Friday night laser shows* are action-packed, using the latest in techno-wizardry.

Age Range: Any age.
Hours: *Museum*–Saturday through Thursday 10:00 A.M. to 5:00 P.M., Friday 10:00 A.M. to 10:00 P.M.
Planetarium Shows–Monday through Friday 2:00 P.M., Friday evening 9:00 P.M. and 11:00 P.M., Saturday and Sunday 12:00 noon and 2:00 P.M.
Laser Light Shows–Friday evening 9:00 P.M. and 11:00 P.M.
Observatory–Friday evening dark to 10:00 P.M.
Admission: *Museum*–Adults $5.00, seniors (62 and over) $3.50, students (13-21) $3.00, children (4-12) $2.00.
Planetarium–$1.75 per person in addition to museum admission.
Laser–9:00 P.M. show $2.00 per person in addition to museum admission; 11:00 P.M. show $4.00.
Observatory–free with museum admission.
Time Allowance: About 1 hour for the museum, 35 minutes for the planetarium.
Directions: From I-95 take the exit for Southern Boulevard and proceed east for 1/4 mile to Parker Boulevard. Turn right on Parker Boulevard and continue until you come to Summit Boulevard. Turn right on Summit Boulevard and follow the signs.
Parking: Free.
Wheelchair Accessible: Yes, except for the observatory. Alternate telescopes are available at lower levels.
Restaurant: No.
Picnicking: Yes.
Rest Rooms: Yes.
Gift Shop: Yes; games, T-shirts, rubber insects.

MORIKAMI MUSEUM AND JAPANESE GARDENS

4000 Morikami Park Road
Delray Beach, FL 33446
(407) 495-0233

FUN SCALE

Copyright © Morikami Museum and Japanese Gardens

Discover a century-old connection between Japan and South Florida. Beginning as a pineapple farming community in the early 1900s, the land has recently been transformed into a 200-acre site that celebrates the living culture of Japan–and in grand style. Spaces include exhibition galleries with quarterly changing exhibits, a theater, an Infotronic Gallery, a Seishin-An Tea House, the Yamato-Kan Museum, and acres upon acres of marvelous gardens.

The museum reflects the Japanese search for inner-peace and tranquillity. Warm wooden walls, slate floors, and arched ceilings surround as you travel through the rooms of Japanese culture, ranging from traditional to modern. Begin with the **IBM Infotronics Gallery**. Touch the "touch screens" and select a category to familiarize yourself with school life, geography, and festivals. Did you know that when students enter the classroom in Japan they take off their shoes and store them in a cabinet for the day? In the other museum galleries, although they generally offer no hands-on activities, are interesting, educational exhibits (for older kids). From kite to toy collections, and kimono displays to carved dragon heads, all are there to learn from. Did you know that the length of kimono sleeve was symbolic? Long sleeves are worn by unmarried women, medium by married women, and short sleeves by men.

The **Yamato-Kan Museum** is smaller, but it holds more kid-friendly activities. Here you'll find a traditional wooden bath, an official tea room, a ten year old's bedroom complete with futon, face-mimicking mirrors, and a huge gong. Take a swing at the gong, but don't forget to take your shoes off before entering!

Experience tasteful splendor of the Japanese. Enter the serene **Zen gardens** and see amazing bonsai trees, ponds filled with golden koi (carp) and giant turtle, and waterfalls. Take a walk on the mile-long nature trail through the pines.

Special programs, which include films and family origami workshops, happen throughout the year. Guided tours can be pre-arranged by calling in advance.

Age Range: 6 and up (minimal hands-on things for younger children). Any age will enjoy the park.
Hours: *Museum*–10:00 A.M. to 5:00 P.M., daily. Closed Mondays and major holidays. *Park*–Sunrise to sundown, daily.
Admission: *Museum*–Adults $4.25, seniors $3.75, children (6-18) $2.00, children under 6 free. Admission to museum is free Sundays from 10:00 A.M. to 12:00 noon. *Parking*–Free.
Time Range: 1 1/2 to 2 hours.
Directions: From I-95 take the exit for Linton Boulevard in Boca Raton. Proceed west for 4 miles and turn left on Carter Road. Go one mile to Morikami Park Road and turn right at the sign.
Parking: Free.
Wheelchair Accessible: Yes.
Restaurant: Cafe only.
Picnicking: Yes.
Rest Rooms: Yes.
Gift Shop: Yes; beautiful tea cups, jewelry, perfumes, T-shirts.

133

ASTRONAUT HALL OF FAME AND SPACE CAMP

**6225 Vectorspace Boulevard
Titusville, FL 32780
(407) 269-6100**

FUN SCALE

Copyright © Astronaut Hall of Fame and Space Camp

Down the road from the Kennedy Space Center you can learn about astronaut history and have fun at the same time. Begin with a time tunnel depicting America's entry into the space race, with Russia's launch of Sputnik and America's launch of Explorer 1. Walk through the tunnel and into the museum, and find space memorabilia, touch-activated informational screens, official try-onable space helmets, a climb-insideable Mercury capsule with John Glenn narrating (have the cameras ready), and a fifteen-minute informational movie of rare film footage which shows twice an hour.

Don't miss taking a trip on **Shuttle to Tomorrow,** a full-scale shuttle orbiter mock-up providing a multi-media trip into the future. You'll learn about the challenges of eating, putting on a space suit, and landing in a micro-gravity situation. Imagine what it's like to be in such extreme temperatures. And your pilot is John Glenn.

Copyright © Astronaut Hall of Fame and Space Camp

Be sure to peek in at the **US Space Camp** activities next door. You're not allowed to partake in the activities

134

Copyright © Astronaut Hall of Fame and Space Camp

unless enrolled as a camper, but they are fun to watch. Have you ever dreamt of becoming an astronaut? If you're between fourth and seventh grades, a seven to ten year old with an accompanying parent, or a professional educator, you can make that dream come true at Space Camp.

Space Camp introduces people to the exciting possibilities of outerspace. Campers train like astronauts on simulators, learn about space science, study rocketry, and explore simulated space shuttle missions using realistic space shuttle and mission control mock-ups.

The heart shrinks in space, making exercise crucial. Pretend to walk on the moon in the *1/6 Chair,* and feel what it would be like to be one-sixth of your normal weight and almost gravityless. Explore the *micro-gravity exercise machines.* Climb into the *Multi Axis Trainer,* which spins on three axes, and leaves you totally out of control—a favorite of the kids. Experience the strength of teamwork and build a group-effort rocket. End the experience with a simulated shuttle mission wearing real space suits. It's an enlightening and fun session, and it may just lead you to a career as a future astronaut.

Age Range: There's a little of something for every one in the Astronaut Hall of Fame, but most exhibits would be more interesting for 8 and up. The Space Camp is designed for fourth through seventh graders unless enrolled in the Parent/Child Space Camp, which is for ages seven through ten accompanied by a parent.
Hours: Open 9:00 a.m. to 5:00 P.M., daily, with extended summer hours. Closed Christmas.
Admission: Adults $7.95, children (4-12) $4.95. Call for Space Camp prices.
Time Allowance: About 3 hours.
Directions: From I-95 take Exit 79 and go east on S.R. 405 for about 4 miles. It's on the right hand side.
Parking: Free.
Wheelchair Accessible: Yes.
Restaurant: Snackbar only.
Picnicking: Yes.
Rest Rooms: Yes.
Gift Shop: Yes, astronaut paraphernalia galore.

BREVARD MUSEUM OF HISTORY AND NATURAL SCIENCE

**2201 Michigan Avenue
Cocoa, FL 32926
(407) 632-1830**

FUN SCALE

A journey through here takes the adventurer a step back in time. Walk through the fifteenth-century Florida Indian hut and enter the museum. See the remains of animals now extinct that once roamed our land. Look at the pottery and beads of the Native Americans. Explore the memorabilia of the Victorian era. Study the collection of mollusks–it's said to be one of the most comprehensive in the world. Look at the time line on the mural, which depicts the Spanish explorers and continues all the way up to the missiles of today.

Aside from the permanent collections, there are quarterly changing exhibits. From **Batter up Brevard**, a baseball display, to **Brain Teasers**, interactive brain-jumbling tests, and **The History of Women**, a you've-come-a-long-way-baby styled exhibit, all will captivate you... to some extent.

The Discovery Room, an interactive area for kids two to six, is a highpoint. Explore the live bee hive and aquarium. Pick up a microphone and hear your voice amplified. Shuffle through some of the shells on the shell shelves. Or walk into the fluorescent light room and watch the colors of your skin and clothes change.

Ask for an *Artie the Armadillo* pamphlet to guide you through twenty-two acres of trails and take you through three different ecosystems of Florida.

Cross the bridge over the swamp and feel the tropical breezes blowing through the Florida hammock. Keep your eyes open for an armadillo, a creature indigenous to American tropics, running about.

Age Range: 3 and up.
Hours: Tuesday through Saturday from 10:00 A.M. to 4:00 P.M., Sunday from 1:00 P.M. to 4:00 P.M.
Admission: Adults $3.00, children (3-17) $1.50.
Time Allowance: 1 to 2 hours.
Directions: From I-95 take Exit 79 and follow S.R. 520 East. Go north on Rt. 1 until Michigan Avenue. Turn west and follow the signs.
Parking: Free.
Wheelchair Accessible: Yes; wheelchairs available.
Restaurant: No.
Picnicking: Yes; there's a covered pavilion.
Rest Rooms: Yes.
Gift Shop: Yes; tote bags, silly T-shirts, rubber snakes.

BREVARD ZOO

8225 North Wickham Road
Melbourne, FL 32940
(407) 254-WILD

FUN SCALE

The recently opened Brevard Zoo is a habitat with a hands-on and environmentally-aware approach to learning about the living creatures with whom we share the planet.

Paws On–The Animal Study Zone is a unique area where kids can learn through play in the hands-on exhibits. The five basic themes are *Bodies*, *Food*, *Senses*, *Homes*, and *Life Over Time (ecology, evolution, and extinction)*. Crawl through the giant soil cube: You'll be sharing it with ants, centipedes, a giant mole coming through the top, and a huge tortoise bursting through the side. Don't worry–the whole construction is made of a soft rubbery material; nothing's alive.

Dig around the partially buried dinosaur fossil in the sand. Walk into the mouth of a full-sized replica of a right whale, which intermittently spouts off. Look out! Measure your speed in the *Who's Faster* activity. Race against computerized times of zebras, skunks, or gators. Climb into the giant spider web or

enormous wooden honeycomb, and look at the live bee hive. Crawl into the giant eagle nest, and peer through the lenses to get a bird's-eye view–compare it with your vision.

Cross the **Amazon River** and the **Tropical Waterfowl Exhibit**, and

step into the wilds of **Latin America**. You'll find a fabulous assortment of animals, including prehensile-tailed porcupines (porcupines with long tails used to hold on to branches), a sleek jaguar named Onyx, red-billed toucans, capybaras (the largest rodents), bobcats, and tapirs with elephant-like snouts. Check out the giant anteater, appropriately named Hoover, after the vacuum cleaners. Don't miss the cotton-topped tamarinds. These cute little monkeys

are brown with wild, white-spiked hair on the tops of their heads, and could easily pass as Tina Turner look alikes. Who does their hair, anyway?

Step into the **Animal Encounter Area** (a.k.a. petting zoo), and get up-close and personal with a wide variety of more cuddly animals. Reach out and pet the bunnies, goats, miniature horses, donkeys, prairie dogs, and alpacas.

Age Range: Any age. Paws On is wonderful for kids 3 to 10.
Hours: 10:00 A.M. to 5:00 P.M., daily.
Admission: Adults $4.00, seniors (60 and up) $3.00, children (2-12) $2.50.
Time Allowance: About 2 hours.
Directions: Take Exit 73 off of I-95 and go east on Wickham Road for about 1/4 mile. Turn right at the sign. You're there.
Parking: Free.
Wheelchair Accessible: Yes. Strollers for rent.
Restaurant: Snackbar only.
Picnicking: Yes.
Rest Rooms: Yes, with changing table.
Gift Shop: Yes.

139

KENNEDY SPACE CENTER
SPACEPORT USA
NASA John F. Kennedy
Space Center, FL 32899
(407) 452-2121

FUN SCALE

Copyright © Kennedy Space Center

Many of the attractions at Spaceport, which is run by the federal government, are free. But if you elect to do either the bus tour or one of the **IMAX** films, the two attractions with a fee, buy your tickets as soon as you

arrive–reservations fill-up quickly.

If you see either of the films–*The Dream is Alive* or *The Blue Planet*–you're in for forty minutes of simulated immersion into spectacular three-dimensional views of the Earth from above. The visuals, realistic sounds, and theater rumblings create real feelings of being in space.

The two-hour bus

tours are divided into two options, both of which take you places the public normally doesn't see. On the Red Tour you may go inside the **Flight Crew Training Building** and experience a simulated Apollo launch countdown in a room with colorful buttons and switches; you may visit the **Vehicle Assembly Building** (the second largest by volume in the world); or you might feel dwarfed next to the **Crawler Transporter** and the official shuttle launch pads. On the Blue Tour, which is more historically oriented and runs weekdays only,

you'll visit **Cape Canaveral Air Force Station**, the **Air force Space Museum**, and **NASA launch sites**. The tours are not geared toward kids, and may even be tedious for the adults, but officials say they are working on a more upbeat, kid-oriented tour for the future.

Taking a bus tour, you'll see Kennedy Space Center is situated on 140,000 acres of a wildlife refuge. Citrus groves with the aroma of orange

Copyright © Kennedy Space Center

blossoms permeate the air. I saw an eagle's nest and, further along, a gator out in the open, lazing in a trench next to one of the NASA buildings. The alligators, I was told, are referred to as the unpaid NASA security force!

All the other things to do and see at the Spaceport are free. The **Rocket Garden** is highlighted by eight authentic rockets and flight hardware which document America's space program. Although nothing in the **Gallery of Manned Spaceflight** is hands-on, it does feature an impressive display of rockets, astronaut memorabilia, and even a moon rock. **Satellites and You** uses high-tech, audio-visual effects and popular media images to show how satellites affect our lives. The presentation lasts about forty-five minutes and might be too long for kids under ten.

Walk over to the **Astronaut Memorial** by the lagoon. The "space mirror" is reminiscent of the Vietnam Memorial in Washington and equally as moving.

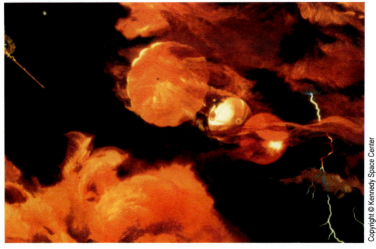

Copyright © Kennedy Space Center

The names of astronauts who gave their lives to research have been inscribed in the black granite slab. The monument stands in the sun's illumination and is controlled by a computer motor aligning it to the sun. The astronaut's names seem to float like stars in the night.

Age Range: 3-5 doubtful, there's not much hands-on; 6-12 the Exploration Station is a must and the IMAX films are fun for those kids who are able to sit still for 40 minutes. Beware: the "tour" is two hours long and certainly not geared toward the younger audience.
Hours: From 9:00 A.M. to 7:00 P.M., daily. Closed on Christmas.
Admission: Bus tour adults $7.00, children (3-11) $4.00. IMAX Theatre adults $4.00, children (3-11) $2.00. All other exhibits are free.
Time Allowance: About 4 hours.
Directions: From I-95 take Exit 79 and go east on State Road 405 and follow signs for Spaceport USA.

Parking: Free.
Wheelchair Accessible: Yes.
Restaurant: Snackbars only..
Picnicking: Yes.
Rest Rooms: Yes.
Gift Shop: Yes.
Cool Tip: Don't miss the underpublicised **Exploration Station**, where family times occur for at least two hours each day. Interact with whisper dishes, a color shadows exhibit, and coordination-testing machines. See the suits that hold the astronauts down while sleeping in a gravityless situation. Try on the heavy lead gloves and experience gravity-overload.

SPACE COAST SCIENCE CENTER AND MUSEUM

1510 Highland Avenue
Melbourne, FL 32936
(407) 259-5572

FUN SCALE

This is a small, exploration-inducing science center loaded with changing exhibits, including **What if I Couldn't...?**, an exhibit designed to sensitize children to disabilities, and **Invaders**, which contains an army of creatures who are pushing the natives of Florida out.

Challenge your mind with interactive physical science exhibits and games. The wonderful **Nature Discovery Room**, a permanent exhibition space, wakens the senses. View, smell, listen to, and even *touch* live creatures in the nature room. If you're lucky, you might be able to hold the endangered black indigo snake. Look at the other creatures such as the pointy-nosed, soft-shelled turtle and green iguana.

The purpose here is to demystify science and, in a small way, the Space Coast Science Center does just that.

Age Range: 3 and up.
Hours: Tuesday through Saturday 10:00 A.M. to 5:00 P.M., Sunday 12:00 noon to 5:00 P.M.
Admission: Adults $3.00, children (ages 3-17) $2.00.
Time Allowance: 1 to 1 1/2 hours.
Directions: Take Exit 72 from I-95 and go east on Eau Gallie Boulevard to Highland Ave and turn left. It's 2 blocks ahead on the left.
Parking: Street parking.
Wheelchair Accessible: Yes.
Restaurant: No.
Picnicking: Yes, across the street.
Rest Rooms: Yes.
Gift Shop: Yes; science games, T-shirts, stuffed animals.

144

THE AUTHENTIC OLD JAIL
167 San Marco Avenue
St. Augustine, FL 32084
(904) 829-3800 or (800) 397-4071

FUN SCALE

Built in 1890, in Victorian Queen Anne architectural style, the Authentic Old Jail served the county up until the 1950s.

Today visitors can take a guided tour through the prison. They run every fifteen minutes and are conducted by "Sheriff Perry" and his wife "Lou." They are dressed in typical late nineteenth-century style clothing and have taken on the roles of their models. Starting in the kitchen where Mrs. Perry cooked meals for the inmates and her family, you're led through the jail–room by room.

In the cell blocks, you'll see minimal furnishings–a bucket and cot. You can contemplate a collection of weapons used both to carry out the crimes and to capture the criminals. Look at the electric chair and also the tree from which people were publicly hanged. Read the actual newspaper accounts of crime, punishment, and events that took place in St. Augustine in the early 1900's.

Age Range: 8 and up.
Hours: 8:30 A.M. to 5:00 P.M., daily. Closed Easter and Christmas.
Admission: Adults $4.25, children (6-12) $3.25.
Time Allowance: 20 or 30 minutes.
Directions: From I-95 take Exit 95 and head east on S.R. 16 until you come to an intersection for U.S. 1. Cross over U.S. 1 and continue for 1 block. Turn right on San Marco Avenue and proceed for about 1 mile. Ahead on the left is St. Augustine Historical Tours and the Authentic Old Jail.
Parking: Free.
Wheelchair Accessible: No.
Restaurant: Snackbar only.
Picnicking: Yes.
Rest Rooms: Yes.
Gift Shop: Yes.

FORT CASTILLO DE SAN MARCOS
1 Castillo Drive
St. Augustine, FL 32084
(904) 829-6506

FUN SCALE

Explore more than three hundred years of Florida history. The roots of the Castillo's history spread from just after Christopher Columbus' discovery of

the New World to today. It was the Spanish who, after defending Florida from both France and Great Britain, realized the need for permanent protection. Thus, between 1672 and 1695, they built this massive fortress.

Through bloody battles, fires, and many historically-significant events, Fort Castillo de San Marcos has stood in full glory on the edge of Matanzas Bay. Cross over the moat and enter the thick coquina-walled (building material made of crushed shells) fortress. The first floor houses the **Powder Magazine** (a vaulted wooden chamber today holding gunpowder, cannon balls, pistols, and Spanish swords), the **Chapel of St. Mark** (a spiritual haven for both soldiers and townspeople), **Storage Rooms**

(to hold ammunition and dried foods), and **Bastions** (diamond-shaped structures positioned so as to create a deadly crossfire between them) at each of the four corners. In the center is a huge courtyard where, occasionally, you'll see flint-lock gun firing demonstrations.

While no guided tours are available, there are twenty-minute ranger talks given throughout the day. The times are randomly scheduled and can be found marked on the clock. Climb the stairs and gaze out at the bay. The fort provides a good aerial view of St. Augustine. Although you're not to climb on the cannons, they are still fun to look at. Cameras ready!

Age Range: Although not much is hands-on at the fort, it would be fun for any adventurers (6 and over) to climb around and imagine themselves defending.
Hours: *Summer*–9:00 A.M. to 6:00 P.M.
Winter–9:00 A.M. to 6:15 P.M.
Admission: Adults (16-61 years old) $2.00, under 16 and over 62 free to U.S. citizens.
Time Allowance: 30 to 60 minutes.
Directions: From I-95 take Exit 95 and head east on S.R. 16 for about 10 miles until you reach U.S. 1. Turn right on U.S. 1 south and continue until you come to King Street. Turn left on King Street and follow it until it ends. Turn left on Castillo Drive and it's ahead on the right. You can't miss it.
Parking: Meter.
Wheelchair Accessible: Yes, on first level only.
Restaurant: No, but nearby.
Picnicking: Yes.
Rest Rooms: Yes.
Gift Shop: Yes; books, prints, war toys.

THE OLDEST WOODEN SCHOOLHOUSE
14 St. George Street
St. Augustine, FL 32084
(904) 824-0192

FUN SCALE

Built over two hundred years ago, the little schoolhouse professes to be the oldest in the USA. Made of cedar and cypress wood, and held together with handmade nails and wooden pegs, it gives a picture of what a schoolhouse was like in the 1800s.

Step inside and witness the schoolhouse come to life. Listen to the animated professor conducting a class. While "Johnny" sits on the side wearing a dunce cap for not doing his homework, others listen attentively as the teacher leads a typical lesson from the mid-nineteenth century. See the "dungeon" under the stairs where unruly children were sent–Is that a rat in the corner? Check out the outdoor privy. Look into the kitchen building. As well as instructing reading, writing, and arithmetic, the teachers maintained vegetable gardens and cooked meals for the children. Drop a penny into the wishing well beneath the ancient pecan tree. (I suggest you wish that you remain in the late twentieth century. Be thankful for the comforts of today!)

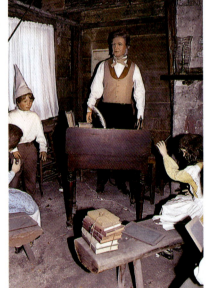

Age Range: School age children (6 and up) will appreciate the schoolhouse.
Hours: 9:00 A.M. to 5:00 P.M. Closed Christmas.
Admission: Adults (13 and up) $1.50, children (6-12) $.75.
Time Allowance: About a half hour.
Directions: From the north, take I-95 south to the Exit for S.R. 16 and continue east, crossing Rt. 1, and turning right on San Marco Avenue. Just past the city gates on your right is St. George Street (the walking street). The schoolhouse is at the beginning on the right.
Parking: Meter or pay-lot.
Wheelchair Accessible: Yes.
Restaurant: No, but nearby.
Picnicking: No.
Rest Rooms: No, but nearby.
Gift Shop: Yes; stationary, post cards, T-shirts.

148

ST. AUGUSTINE HISTORICAL TOURS

167 San Marco Avenue (Route A1A)
St. Augustine, FL 32084
(904) 829-3800

FUN SCALE

While there are a number of ways see St. Augustine, one particularly pleasant option is a sightseeing-trolley tour. Hop on a green and white open-air vehicle that takes you on a narrated journey. It's a great way to eliminate parking problems and enjoy a leisurely tour through the city. You're able to get off and on the trolley at the various stops along the way, and tickets are good for three consecutive days. Stops include: Authentic Old Jail, Ripley's Believe It or Not!, Oldest Wooden Schoolhouse, Zorayda Castle, Fountain of Youth, and Potters Wax Museum.

Age Range: Any age can use the trolley for transportation purposes. As a non-stop tour, 10 and up may most appreciate it.
Hours: 8:20 A.M. to 5:00 P.M., daily.
Admission: Adults $10.00, children (6-12) $4.00. Prices don't include admission to attractions, but "package tours" are available.
Time Allowance: The tour, without stopping, lasts for an hour.
Directions: From I-95 take Exit 95 and go east on S.R. 16 until you come to an intersection for U.S. 1. Cross over U.S. 1 and continue for one block. Turn right on San Marco Avenue and proceed for about one mile. Ahead on the left is St. Augustine Historical Tours and the Authentic Old Jail.
Parking: Free.
Wheelchair Accessible: No.
Restaurant: Yes.
Picnicking: Yes.
Rest Rooms: Yes.
Gift Shop: Yes.

149

POTTER'S WAX MUSEUM
17 King Street
St. Augustine, FL 32084
(904) 829-9056

FUN SCALE

To the left as you enter, you're immediately confronted by a fierce-looking *Rambo* and a wild-eyed *Freddie Kruger*. To the right is *Sleeping Beauty,* with her chest mechanically breathing up and down. The figures are startlingly life-like. Even the hair is real–it's added strand by strand when a figure is created. Potter's Wax Museum, built in 1940, was the first of its kind in America.

Continue inside and tour through the galleries with 170 authentically dressed and meticulously sculptured figures of historical importance. Meet up with *Marco Polo* and *Queen Victoria.* It's easy to imagine the figure of *John F. Kennedy* coming to life right before your eyes. Stay away from the *Torture Room* if you're weak-stomached; it contains some pretty gory figures. One of the museum's highlights is the moving *Frankenstein.* Push a button to activate the electric sparks and bubbles that begin in the bolt on his neck and travel throughout his massive body. Watch out, he lurches forward as if he's coming at you!

Step into the multi-image presentation in the theater and experience a

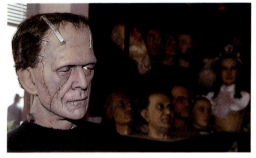

twelve-minute film that occurs every twenty minutes. You're taken on a boat trip, through a boy's dreams, into the lives of some of history's greats. The boy looks in on Beethoven and Columbus and realizes that he, too, has the potential to do great feats.

Age Range: 8 and up. The only "touchables" are the wax figures in the front.
Hours: *Summer*–9:00 A.M. to 8:00 P.M.
Winter–9:00 A.M. to 5:00 P.M.
Admission: Adults $5.00, seniors $4.25, children (7-12) $2.75.
Time Allowance: 30 to 45 minutes.
Directions: From I-95 take Exit 95 and head east on S.R. 16 for about 10 miles until you reach U.S. 1. Turn right on U.S. 1 south until you come to King Street. Turn left on King Street and it's ahead on the right.
Parking: Meter.
Wheelchair Accessible: Yes.
Restaurant: No, but nearby.
Picnicking: No, but nearby.
Rest Rooms: Yes, with changing table in woman's.
Gift Shop: Yes; T-shirts, statues, postcards.

151

ST. AUGUSTINE ALLIGATOR FARM
999 Anastasia Boulevard
St. Augustine, FL 32085
(904) 824-3337

FUN SCALE

There's evidence of Crocodilia (gators and crocs) having been around seven million years ago. Well, St. Augustine Alligator Farm hasn't been around for quite as long, but it *did* open way back in 1893. Listed in the National Register of Historic Places, it's Florida's oldest continuously operating attraction and certainly the oldest gator farm.

The approach to gator exhibition here is less sensationalistic than at some of the other gator farms. There are no gator ribs or nuggets at the snack bar, and they don't tell you startling, truly unbelievable gator facts. There is, however, a breathtaking collection of gators and crocs of all shapes, sizes, and nationalities, as well as other fascinating creatures.

Don't miss the two regularly scheduled shows–the **Reptile Show** and the **Alligator Show**. They're twenty minutes in length and hold the interest of even the three-year-olds. The Reptile Show teaches, among other things, how to tell the difference between venomous and non-venomous snakes. In the other show, hear the baby gators "aarkpp." The shows are each full of snake and gator facts. And you're able to hold, in your very own two hands, a group of snakes after the Reptile Show and a baby gator after the Alligator Show. Cameras ready!

Stroll through the park and check out the complete collection of Crocodilia. It is grouped geographically and covers every type. Certainly the most startlingly eye-opening reptile is Gomek, the huge, and I mean *huge* with a capital H, saltwater crocodile. Gomek is about eighteen feet long and weighs some eighteen hundred pounds. He's the largest in captivity and is around fifty years old. He spends his mornings dipping in the water and the rest of the day

Copyright © St. Augustine Alligator Farm

lounging on the bank. Absolutely massive, Gomek has made it into the *Guiness Book of World Records*.

There's a **petting zoo** with Fallow deer, Nubian goats, and Mouflon sheep. Of course it isn't as exciting as seeing Gomek, but then there's nothing pettable about Gomek.

Discover real Florida as you stroll along the elevated boardwalk through the gator swamp in **Florida's Natural Habitat**. See the gators lazing in the sun catching some rays. Look up and see the wild egret, ibis, and wood stork birds nesting and feeding in the park's tropical foliage, and surveying the situation from above.

St. Augustine Alligator Farm provides informative learning and entertainment in an atmosphere of respect for living creatures (no matter how scary looking), with emphasis on environmental awareness. Kudos!

Age Range: 3 and up. There's a petting zoo for kids 3 to 5, and they might enjoy touching the snake and gators after the shows. *Any* age is awed by Gomek.
Hours: 10:00 A.M. to 5:00 P.M., daily.
Admission: Adults $8.95, seniors (65 and up) 10 percent discount, children (3-10) $5.95.
Time Allowance: 2 1/2 to 3 hours.
Directions: From I-95 take Exit 95 and head east on S.R. 16 for about 10 miles until you reach U.S. 1. Turn right on U.S. 1 south and continue until you come to King Street. Turn left on King Street and follow it until the end. Cross the Bridge of Lions and continue on A1A south. It's about 2 miles ahead on the right.
Parking: Free.
Wheelchair Accessible: Yes.
Restaurant: Snackbar only.
Picnicking: Yes.
Rest Rooms: Yes.
Gift Shop: Yes.

ST. AUGUSTINE'S RIPLEY'S BELIEVE IT OR NOT!

19 San Marco Avenue
St. Augustine, FL 32085
(904) 824-1606

FUN SCALE

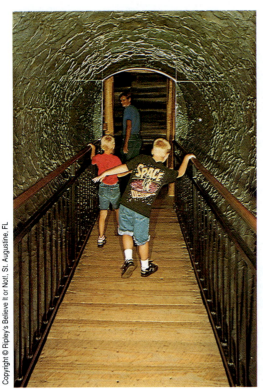

Copyright © Ripley's Believe It or Not!, St. Augustine, FL

Housed in the 1887 Moorish Revival style castle, St. Augustine's Ripley's Believe It or Not! seems only moderately out of place. It exists in the oldest town in the USA and is surrounded by history. What better place for a somewhat bizarre display of unbelievable discoveries!

Enter the museum and you're immediately greeted by a life-size man and his mule made of pure junk–old toys, kitchen utensils, and other discarded items. Continue up the staircase and explore three floors of exhibits designed to stir your curiosity. The collection–believe it or not–originates from every corner of the Earth.

See hard-to-believe, yet tastefully-designed displays ranging from blades of rice, complete with the entire "Lord's Prayer" handwritten on them, to the stuffed "Beauregard," the world's only six-legged cow. Come face-to-face with a genuine Jivaro shrunken head from Equador. Be dwarfed by the twenty-four-foot model of the Eiffel Tower made of 110,000 toothpicks. Don't believe it? I dare you to count. Observe the "genuine" Fiji Island mermaid. Look at the world's most famous painting–"The Mona Lisa"–but this version is created solely from sixty-three slices of toast. (Now that's culture!)

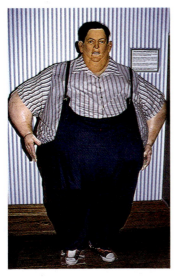

Don't be surprised if the bridge that you're standing on as you gaze out at the gators unexpectedly drops from beneath you. And don't be surprised to find the two-way mirror with people unknowingly making ridiculous faces on the other side. Exiting the museum, you will pass through a spinning tunnel that leaves you dizzy for days.

Believe it, or not? Well, maybe not...

Age Range: 6 and up.
Hours: *Winter*–9:00 A.M. to 6:00 P.M., daily.
Summer–9:00 A.M. to 9:00 P.M., daily.
Admission: Adults $7.50, seniors $5.50, children (5-12) $4.25.
Time Allowance: About an hour.
Directions: From I-95 take Exit 95 and head east on S.R. 16 until you come to an intersection for U.S. 1. Cross over U.S. 1 and continue for one block. Turn right on San Marco Avenue and continue for about 1 mile. It's on your left.
Parking: Free.
Wheelchair Accessible: First-floor only. Free admittance.
Restaurant: No.
Picnicking: Yes, with canopy.
Rest Rooms: Yes.
Gift Shop: Yes; T-shirts, games, cool umbrellas.

155

MARINELAND

**9507 Oceanshore Boulevard
Marineland, FL 32086
(904) 471-1111 or (800) 824-4218**

FUN SCALE

Established in 1938, Marineland is the world's oldest oceanarium. From the outside it appears to be less flashy and up-to-date than some of its more modern competitors, but it has a certain down-to-earth quality I found refreshing.

Through extensive ocean research, the staff has created spectacular shows and exhibits. Although known mostly for their dolphin shows, there are other sea creatures as well.

Educated Dolphins, originating in the 1950's, was the first trained dolphin show. It's twenty minutes of educated dolphin tricks and maneuvers. See bottlenose dolphins play baseball, basketball, football, and jump through hoops. By the way, the oldest dolphin in captivity is forty-one year old "Nellie" and she lives here.

The **Jumping Dolphins** show is a spectacular, short but sweet performance. The ten-minute show has dolphins doing triple flips as high as sixteen feet in the air. See the **Sea Lion Training** program where the mammals do all kinds of tricks. Have you ever seen a 600-pound sea lion balance on one flipper? Also, watch the penguins eat from the hands of trainers during **Tropical Penguin Feeding**. Listen to a ten-minute educational talk on the life of a penguin.

The **electric eel display** is okay to avoid altogether. The sad looking slimy creatures live in a small, grungy tank and are surrounded by obnoxious electrical sound effects blaring over the loudspeaker. The electric eel can grow to five feet in length and generate up to 600 volts of electricity. Ouch!

Step into the **Aquarius Theater** and experience a twenty-two minute, 3-D film about sea life. *Sea Dream* creates an illusion of sea creatures that appear to come off the screen at you. (Look out!) In **Play Port,** kids two to eleven let loose. Jump in the *Air Bounce Bag*. Kick the swinging bags in *Bag Tag*. Go up the ropes on the *Rope Climb*. Or, relax!

Age Range: 3 and 4 year olds may find the lack of a touch tank or anything touchable a big disappointment, but they will appreciate the fantastic water shows.
Hours: 9:00 A.M. to 5:30 P.M., daily.
Admission: Adults $12.00, seniors 20 percent discount, students (12-18) $9.00, children (3-11) $7.00.
Time Allowance: About 3 hours to see all of the shows and exhibits.
Directions: Traveling *north* on I-95 take Exit 93 (S.R. 206) and go east to A1A. Turn right on A1A and continue south for 7 miles.
Traveling *south* on I-95, take Exit 91 (S.R. 100) and go east on S.R. 100 until it ends. Turn left on A1A and continue north for 12 miles.
Parking: Free.
Wheelchair Accessible: Yes, all but top deck shows. Port hole views are available from below. Wheelchairs are loaned at no charge; Strollers are rented for a fee.
Restaurant: Yes.
Picnicking: Yes, in specified areas.
Rest Rooms: Yes.
Gift Shop: Yes, T-shirts, stationary, bumper stickers.

157

ART CONNECTIONS
AT CUMMER GALLERY
829 Riverside Avenue
Jacksonville, FL 32204
(904) 355-0630

FUN SCALE

How do kids make sense of art? They step into **Art Connections**, an interactive gallery based on the original works in the Cummer collection, and experiment. Here you can explore many of the choices an artist makes while creating; art materials, art technology, and imagination come together and begin to make sense.

Stand inside a *camera obscura* and think about early forms of recording light. Draw yourself on top of a painting. Explore the world of computers and make a computer-art masterpiece. Experiment with different textures and think about how they contribute to an image. See your own body change colors on a gigantic shadow screen. Step into a painting and imagine living in that time period. Art Connections is fun for all ages, and is considered a prototype and inspiration to other galleries.

The **Cummer Gallery of Art** alone, although not as much fun for kids as Art Connections, is definitely worth investigating. The gallery collection consists of work from 2000 B.C. to the present and includes more than two thousand pieces. While known for its eighteenth-century Meissen porcelain collection, the gallery also displays paintings, sculptures, furniture, and graphics. The gallery is surrounded by glorious Italian gardens outside modeled after a villa

Copyright © Cummer Gallery

near Florence. Step into the gardens and gaze out at the St. John's River. Stroll past sprinkling fountains, vine-covered fences, and archways. Ignore the sky scrapers and pretend you're in Italy. Why not?

Age Range: Any age will enjoy Art Connections. The Gallery is more interesting for older kids (8 and up).
Hours: Tuesday through Friday from 10:00 A.M. to 4:00 P.M., Saturday from 12:00 noon to 5:00 P.M., Sunday from 2:00 P.M. to 5:00 P.M. Closed Monday.
Admission: Adults $3.00, children and students (5-18) $1.00, seniors and military $2.00.
Time Allowance: About 2 hours.
Directions: From the *south*, take I-95 North to College Street (Exit 110). Return to southbound I-95 and Riverside Avenue (Exit 109). Turn right on Riverside for 1/2 block.
From the *north*, take I-95 South to Riverside Avenue (Exit 109). Turn right on Riverside for 1/2 block.
Parking: Free.
Wheelchair Accessible: Yes.
Restaurant: No.
Picnicking: Yes.
Rest Rooms: Yes, with changing tables.
Gift Shop: Yes; T-shirts, various objets d'art, jewelry.

JACKSONVILLE'S MUSEUM OF SCIENCE AND HISTORY

**1025 Museum Circle
Jacksonville, FL 32207
(904) 396-7062**

FUN SCALE

Spark your curiosity. The Museum of Science and History (MOSH) interprets the history, natural history, and science of northeast Florida by providing both the stimulus and outlet for curious visitors.

The **Bryan Science Theatre** is the place for hair-raising and interactive experiences. See physical science demonstrations, live animal programs, and other amazing displays. Learn about electricity, motion, sound, and physical body phenomena through extraordinary hands-on activities.

The **Living World and the Living Room** contain native live specimens. Housed in a twelve-hundred-gallon marine aquarium live a colorful variety of Florida ocean creatures including sea urchins, star fish, and fiddler crabs. Step into the aviary and listen to the Florida songbirds serenade.

Kidspace allows for a child's very first experience in science. Children under forty-eight inches tall can explore a water table. Splash around with the water wheel and test an item's floatability. They can paint each other's faces, put on puppet shows, play in a two-story tree house, and fill miniature cars with make-believe gasoline from real gas pumps. This is a healthy and safe environment for discovery and learning.

Check out the permanent, but often-added-to, *Maple Leaf* exhibit. The *Maple Leaf* sunk in 1865 in the St. John's River. Because the ship settled in mud, she's well preserved. The ongoing excavation continues to reveal valuable artifacts.

Geared toward both adults and children, the **Alexander Brest Planetarium** provides a ride on a comet through our solar system and a spin around the center of a distant galaxy. Through the MOSH's special sound system, you'll feel a shuttle launch and clearly hear a whisper muttered in outerspace. The special projection system allows you to see stars and other universal bodies–as if you were right there. Along with the regular planetarium shows, Kidstar productions, tailored to the younger audience, are also featured.

Age Range: All ages.

Hours: Monday through Friday 10:00 A.M. to 5:00 P.M., Saturday 10:00 A.M. to 6:00 P.M., Sunday 1:00 to 6:00 P.M. Closed New Year's, Thanksgiving, and Christmas. September hours vary. Call for details.

Admission: Adults $5.00, seniors and children (4-12) $3.00. Admission fees include planetarium.

Time Allowance: 3 to 5 hours.

Directions: Traveling *south* on I-95, take the exit for I-10 west. Cross the Fuller Bridge and follow the signs. Traveling *north* on I-95, take the exit for Prudential Drive and follow the signs.

Parking: Free.

Wheelchair Accessible: Yes.

Restaurant: No, nearby.

Picnicking: Yes, with tables.

Rest Rooms: Yes, with changing tables in some of the rest rooms.

Gift Shop: Yes; T-shirts, telescopes, kites.

JACKSONVILLE ZOOLOGICAL PARK
8605 Zoo Road
Jacksonville, FL 32218
(904) 757-4463

FUN SCALE

Discover the wonders of wildlife through some eight hundred animals that inhabit this park–from African antelopes to dwarf zebus.

Listen to the call of the wild. Take a safari through the eleven-acre **African Veldt**. Travel down the boardwalk through ostriches, antelopes, and gazelles.

Turn down another boardwalk and experience the **Okavango Trail**. You will see animals typically found in the Okavango River region of southern Africa, including blue duikers, dik-diks, and African crocodiles. Check out the walk-through **aviary** of exotic birds, then gaze across the water to the **Chimpanorama**. Watch the silly chimps play together on their own island.

At **Mahali Pa Simba** you'll witness many roaming lions. See lions sleep, stretch, yawn, and gnaw on raw meat treats. *Mahali pa simba* means "the place of the lion" in Swahili.

Learn something about the **Florida Wetlands** as you meander along the boardwalk, winding through the natural wetlands. See a lush habitat packed with plants and animals indigenous to Florida. Discover the **Outdoor Aviary** where marabou storks and Pondicherry vultures fly freely about the enclosure.

Small children will go wild over **Okvango Village Petting Zoo**. Reach out and stroke domestic African animals. Pet pygmy donkeys, dwarf zebus,

Copyright © Jacksonville Zoo

and miniature horses–to name just a few.

Copyright © Jacksonville Zoo

Learn about the largest living land mammal in *"Elephant Encounter."* Here is a chance to have a close-up elephant encounter and have your questions answered by elephant experts. Times for the half-hour demonstration are posted at the front gate and Elephant Exhibit.

"Can We Talk... Animals" offers another close-up view of a daily animal and discussion with the zoo keeper. It's possible to reach out and even *touch* some of the animals in the program. Located across the path from the zebras, "Can We Talk... Animals" takes place from 12:00 noon to 1:00 P.M. and from 2:00 to 3:00 P.M., Wednesday through Sunday.

"Let's Talk... Animals" is a more ecologically-oriented show where a mammal, reptile, or bird is encouraged to exhibit its natural behavior. For instance, the baby giant anteater clings to a towel for dear life. She does this because in the wild, for security, she would hold onto her mother's back for the first few months of her life. Shows happen at 11:00 A.M., 1:30 P.M., and 3:30 P.M., on weekends and holidays.

Crocodile and Alligator Feeding takes place at 2:00 P.M. on Saturdays during the warm weather months.

For an additional $1.50, you can hop on the **mini-train** and take a tour around the zoo. All aboard!

Age Range: Any age.
Hours: 9:00 A.M. to 5 P.M., daily. Closed Thanksgiving, Christmas, and New Year's Day.
Admission: Adults $4.00. seniors (65 and over) $3.00, children (12 and under) $2.50. Wheelchair and stroller rentals available for $1.50.
Time Allowance: 2 or 3 hours.
Directions: From I-95 take Exit 124-A (Heckscher Drive). Cross S.R. 17 and it's on the right.
Parking: Free.
Wheelchair Accessible: Yes.
Restaurant: Snackbar only.
Picnicking: Yes, with tables.
Rest Rooms: Yes, with changing tables.
Gift Shop: Yes; T-shirts, stuffed animals, post cards.

WAKULLA SPRINGS STATE PARK
One Spring Drive
Wakulla Springs, FL 32305
(904) 922-3633

FUN SCALE

Copyright © Wakulla Springs

Wakulla Springs State Park–the 2,860-acre home of one of the world's largest and deepest fresh water springs–gives you a chance to observe nature at its finest. The Wakulla Spring, itself, is huge–almost three acres. It's a constant seventy degrees year-round. **Glassbottom Boat Tours** afford the chance to see–one hundred feet below, in the mouth of the cavern–lush underwater vegetation, fish, and even a few fossilized mastodon bones. The Ice Age mammal's remains were found by scientists scavenging around the depths of the spring. Tours are given from 10:30 A.M. to 3:30 P.M., daily, when the water is clear enough, and last about a half-hour.

Hike along the six-miles of hiking trails. The park is a popular birding mecca. Shallow marshes and hardwood forests provide a rich natural habitat for purple gallinules, American coots, osprey, and turkey vultures, among many other feathered friends.

Afterwards, take a dip in the designated swimming area near the spring. Partake in a ranger-led snorkeling program. They're offered during the warmer months and reservations are required.

Riverboat Tours also last for a half-hour and run daily from 9:30 A.M. to 5:00 P.M. During the two-mile journey, you'll see plenty of alligators, birds, turtles and, occasionally, deer and wild turkeys.

The **Lodge and Conference Center**, built in 1937 and ornately

164

decorated, offers overnight accommodations, a dining room, snackbar, and gift shop. Camping is also available. For information call (904) 224-5950.

Age Range: Any age.
Hours: 6:00 A.M. to sunset, daily.
Admission: *Park*–$3.25 per vehicle and up to eight people. Each Additional passenger is $1.00. Pedestrians and cyclists are $1.00.
Glassbottom Boat or River Tours–Adults $4.50, children $2.25.
Leashed pets are allowed in certain areas.
Time Allowance: 2 hours to full day.
Directions: From I-10 take the exit for Highway 319 in Tallahassee. Proceed south on I-319 and exit on S.R. 61. At the intersection of S.R. 61 and S.R. 267 turn left. The entrance is ahead on the right.
Parking: $3.25 per vehicle.
Wheelchair Accessible: Yes; on boats also. Trails are bumpy.
Restaurant: Yes, dining room in lodge and snackbar. Reservations advisable for dining room.
Picnicking: Yes, with grills.
Rest Rooms: Yes, with changing tables near swimming area and lodge.
Gift Shop: Yes; T-shirts, stuffed animals, puzzles.

SPECIAL BEACHES

Sandy beaches cover 1,016 miles of Florida's 8,000-mile, tidal shoreline, the longest of any state other than Alaska. While there *are* a lot of beaches in Florida, a few stand out in my mind.

VENICE PUBLIC BEACH
Venice Avenue, Venice, FL
(813) 488-4458

Venice, Florida, actually has more canals than its namesake in Italy. The most interesting part of *this* Venice lies not within its canals, but on its beaches. Several stories account for why so many shark's teeth are found here. One says there was an ancient shark burial ground just offshore. Another, perhaps more realistically, proposes the abundance of teeth is the result of the shape of the gulf's floor and water currents. Today, you can look down at the sand and, after adjusting your eyes, see black shark's teeth scattered throughout the broken shells.

This is a great place to spend the day gazing down and shuffling through the sand. When I asked a British couple if they had found any teeth yet, they were dumbfounded, so I explained why everyone was walking with their heads down. The man replied with an English accent, "I thought everyone was just sad." (Oh, those silly Brits!)

By the way, the teeth are black not because they're dead or ancient, but because of their reaction to salt water. So why don't living sharks have mouths full of black teeth? If you look into a shark's mouth (be careful!), you'll see multiple layers of teeth, all white. Sharks regularly lose them before they turn black, and regrow new ones. They come in pearly white.

Hours: The beaches are never closed. Lifeguards are at Venice Public Beach from 10:00 A.M. to 4:15 P.M., daily.
Admission: Free. No pets, however, are allowed on any of the beaches.
Directions: From I-75 take Exit 35 for Venice. Follow Jacaranda Boulevard until you see Venice Avenue. Turn right on Venice Avenue and follow it for about seven miles. Cross the bridge (you're still on Venice Avenue) and continue for another mile.

Parking: Free.
Restaurant: Snackbars only.
Picnicking: Yes. No glass containers.
Rest Rooms: Yes, with showers.
Cool Tip: If you can't find any shark's teeth on the beach, take a drive to the Clearwater Science Center. Little bags of shark's teeth are sold in the gift shop. For about a dollar you get approximately ten teeth, and the science center is worth a peek.

SANIBEL ISLAND BEACHES
Sanibel Island, FL
(813) 472-3700 (town hall)

Grab your shell pail, hit the beach at low tide or after a storm, and you're in for some stupendous shelling. Sanibel Island has the reputation of being one of the world's finest spots to scavenge for shells; its position, relative to gulf winds and tides, accounts for this. The sand is soft and white, and the water aqua blue. There are collectibles galore, ranging from pea tubes and sand dollars to whelks and sharks' eyes.

By the way, look for the "unliving" shells (those that are open). The ones that are closed, most likely, have something alive inside. There's a law that states that only two live shells per species per person may be taken. It makes sense–otherwise the sensational shell collecting won't last long.

There are a number of beautiful beaches surrounding the island. Drive around, find a legal place to park, and–happy beaching! There are no lifeguards at any of the beaches.

Hours: Always.
Admission: Free, but bridge toll fee is $3.00 per car (round trip).
Pets allowed on beaches.
Directions: Traveling north on I-75, take the exit for Daniel's Road (south of Fort Myers) and follow signs. Traveling south on I-75, take the exit for S.R. 884 and follow the signs.
Parking: Free, but limited.
Restaurant: No.
Picnicking: Yes.
Rest Rooms: Yes, on some. No shower facilities available.

LUMMUS PARK BEACH
SOUTH BEACH, MIAMI BEACH

Thirteenth Street and Ocean Drive, South Miami Beach, FL
(305) 673-7714

Running along Ocean Drive from Fifth through Fourteenth Streets in the art deco district of South Miami Beach reveals a gem of a find. Don't think that you'll be the only one to *find* this beach though–it's a popular spot!

If you're into chic, go to Lummus Park Beach. It's on South Beach in Miami Beach, alongside the tastefully-restored art deco district. Here heavily tanned, beautiful athletic types roller blade along the boardwalk wearing teensy bathing suits, people fly kites on the beach, and sunbathers bask in the sun alongside the deep blue sea. As well as splashing in the water and building sand castles, children frolic in the relatively new play area next to the beach at Thirteenth Street and Ocean Drive. Take some time to eat in the assortment of ethnic eateries. It's an action-packed spot and fun for all ages.

Hours: The beach is always open.

Admission: Free. Lifeguards are scattered along the beach from 9:00 A.M. until 5:00 P.M., daily, during the warm weather months. No pets allowed on beaches.

Directions: From I-95 take the exit for I-195 and head east across the Biscayne Bay on the Julia Tuttle Causeway. Proceed until you come to A1A (Collins Avenue). Turn right and go south until you come to 14th Street. Turn left and drive one block until you reach the beach. Turn right on Ocean Drive and begin the search for a meter or parking lot.

Parking: Meter and pay-lot.

Restaurant: Many.

Picnicking: Yes.

Rest Rooms: Yes.

ST. AUGUSTINE BEACHES
Anastasia Island, FL
(904) 471-1596

You will find an expansive stretch of stark-white sand here, bordered by the deep-blue sea on one side and massive sand dunes on the other. The sand is packed hard enough for cars to drive, mountain bikers to ride, and runners to run on; closer to the water, it's softer and perfect for sunbathers to lie in. These beaches are less crowded and wider than those further south in Florida. St. Augustine Beach begins at the northern tip of Anastasia Island and continues–for twenty-four miles–all the way down to Marineland.

A word of warning. Heed the signs about not swimming in certain areas where there are dangerous currents.

Hours: The beach is always open. Lifeguards are on duty from 10:00 A.M. to 5:00 P.M., daily.
Admission: Free. Pets allowed if on a leash.
Directions: From St. Augustine, cross the Bridge of Lions and follow A1A south. Choose your beach. I would suggest parking in the lot just north of the Howard Johnson's Motel and walking north along the beach until you come to the life guarded area. It's a nice walk.
Parking: Free. Lots are at Butler Beach, Crescent Beach, and next to the Howard Johnson's Motel.
Restaurant: Yes, many.
Picnicking: Yes, but no glass containers are allowed.
Rest Rooms: Yes.
Cool Tip: During certain times of the year, the Portuguese Man of War invades the Atlantic coast. Don't be fooled by these neon, aqua-colored balloons with colored strings hanging from below. Although they may *look* tempting to pick up and pop on the beach, they sting: You'll experience a burning sensation that will last for hours if you touch one. If you *do* get stung, try putting a mixture of baking soda and water on the burn.

BASEBALL SPRING TRAINING
(See addresses below)

Pitches fly, bats crack, baseballs thump in gloves... and excitement permeates the air. Have you ever wanted to see your team's favorite players up-close, get an autograph, and see them doing warm-ups? It's possible, and even free, every spring in Florida. Late February marks the beginning of spring training for about two-thirds of the major league teams. Scattered throughout Florida are twenty teams that warm up for two weeks before the exhibition games. These games in the "Grapefruit League" are played daily, through March. A spectator told me that one of his fondest growing-up memories was when he and his father came here to watch the Red Sox.

A typical day of spring training begins at 9:00 a.m., when the players dress and hold a team meeting. At 10:00 they do warm-up exercises, followed by off-mound drills and a break. You can see pitchers start to throw at 11:15, and the players begin batting and catching practice at 11:30. Pitchers do physical conditioning at 11:45, and the players call it a day around 2:00 p.m.–which leaves plenty of time for them to meet their fans. Don't expect to

find an organized tour (or a date with Michael Jordan) at each of the sites, but you *can* expect to see some of your favorite players on a more personal level than during the regular season. Who knows, maybe you *will* score a talk with Roger Clemens!

170

Spring Training Sites in Florida

Atlanta Braves–West Palm Beach. Phone (407) 683-6100.
Baltimore Orioles–St. Petersburg. Phone (813) 894-4773.
Boston Red Sox–Fort Myers. Phone (813) 334-4700.
Chicago White Sox–Sarasota. Phone (813) 366-8451.
Cincinnati Reds–Plant City. Phone (813) 752-7337.
Cleveland Indians–Winter Haven. Phone (813) 293-3900.
Detroit Tigers–Lakeland. Phone (813) 499-8229.
Florida Marlins–Melbourne. Phone (407) 633-9200.
Houston Astros–Kissimmee. Phone: (407) 933-2520.
Kansas City Royals–Haines City. Phone (813) 424-2500.
Los Angeles Dodgers–Vero Beach. Phone (407) 569-4900.
Minnesota Twins–Fort Myers. Phone (800) 288-9467.
Montreal Expos–West Palm Beach. Phone (407) 689-9121.
New York Mets–Port Saint Lucie. Phone (407) 871-2115.
New York Yankees–Fort Lauderdale. Phone (305) 776-1921.
Philadelphia Phillies–Clearwater. Phone (813) 442-8496.
Pittsburgh Pirates–Braedenton. Phone (813) 748-4610.
Saint Louis Cardinals–St. Petersburg. Phone (813) 896-4641.
Texas Rangers–Port Charlotte. Phone (813) 625-9500.
Toronto Blue Jays–Dunedin. Phone: (813) 733-0429.

Age Range: Any age, as long as a baseball fan.
Hours: From around February 19 until the beginning of April. Practice times 10:00 A.M. until 2:00 P.M., daily, for the first two weeks. Games take place during March. Call for more information.
Admission: Spring Training workouts are free to watch, but there is a fee for the games; however, it's nominal in comparison with the price of games during baseball season.
Time Allowance: About 2 hours.
Cool Tip: Go armed with autographable baseballs. Don't forget the pen!

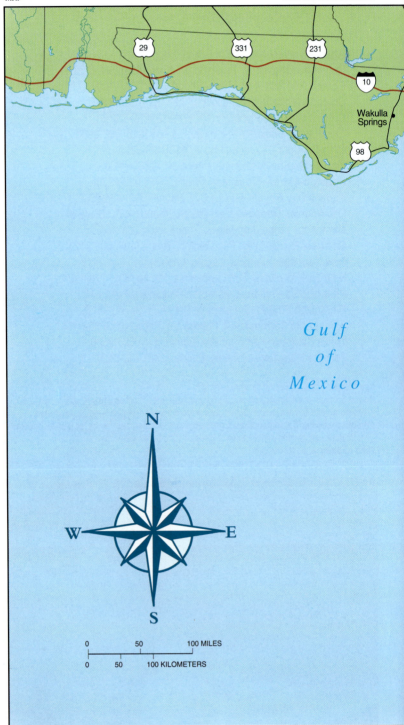

ATLANTIC OCEAN

Jacksonville

St. Augustine

Orlando

Cocoa Beach

Kissimmee

Tampa

Clearwater

Winter Haven

St. Petersburg

Sarasota

Punta Gorda

Fort Meyers

Naples

West Palm Beach

Delray Beach

Boca Raton

Fort Lauderdale

Miami

Key West

INDEX

174